Phonological Awareness Assessment and Instruction

A Sound Beginning

Sally Barnhart

Holly B. Lane

University of Florida

Paige C. Pullen

University of Virginia

PEARSON

Boston   New York   San Francisco
Mexico City   Montreal   Toronto   London   Madrid   Munich   Paris
Hong Kong   Singapore   Tokyo   Cape Town   Sydney

Series Editor: *Aurora Martinez Ramos*
Series Editorial Assistant: *Erin Beatty*
Marketing Manager: *Elizabeth Fogarty*
Composition and Prepress Buyer: *Linda Cox*
Manufacturing Manager: *Andrew Turso*
Cover Coordinator: *Joel Gendron*
Editorial-Production Coordinator: *Mary Beth Finch*
Editorial-Production Service: *Stratford Publishing Services*
Electronic Composition: *Stratford Publishing Services*
Illustrator: *Sandra Lindfors*

For related titles and support materials, visit our online catalog at www.ablongman.com

Between the time Website information is gathered and then published, it is not unusual for some sites to have closed. Also, the transcription of URLs can result in unintended typographical errors. The publisher would appreciate notification where these errors occur so that they can be corrected in subsequent editions.

Library of Congress Cataloging-in-Publication Data

Lane, Holly B.
    A sound beginning : phonological awareness assessment and instruction / Holly B. Lane,
Paige C. Pullen.
        p.   cm.
    Includes bibliographical references and index.
    ISBN 0-205-39234-2
    I. Reading—Phonetic method. Title: Phonological awareness assessment and instruction.
II. Pullen, Paige C.   III. Title.

    LB1573.3.L28   2004
    372.46'5—dc21   2003052284

Printed in the United States of America
10 9 8 7 6 5 4 3 2 1   08 07 06 05 04 03

Contents

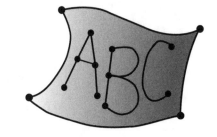

CHAPTER SEVEN

The Phoneme Level 66

Phonemic Awareness   67

Phoneme Level Assessment   69

Phoneme Level Activities   69

Activities

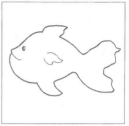

Preface

This book is the result of our own research and of our work with teachers. Although much new knowledge has been generated in recent years about the nature and importance of phonological awareness in the development of reading ability, the application of this knowledge in classroom instruction has been sparse. Many children continue to struggle to learn to read, because they have been provided little or no instruction in phonological awareness. We hope that this book will improve reading outcomes for some of those children.

We spend much of our time teaching teachers to teach reading. Many of the preservice and practicing teachers with whom we have worked have indicated that, although they had heard that phonological awareness was important, they never understood why or what to do about it. We developed this book to provide teachers with a source of information about why phonological awareness is important and what they can do about it. We provide teachers with an overview of the latest research on phonological awareness and methods for assessment and instruction. The book is intended primarily for teachers of children in preschool through grade three, although teachers of older, struggling readers should also find it useful.

We wish to acknowledge several individuals who made important contributions to the development of this book: our editor, Aurora Martinez, and her assistant, Katie Freddoso; Sandra Lindfors, the artist who created our illustrations; and LuAnn Jordan, who wrote the stories for the Robbie the Robot activity. We would also like to thank Jeanne Cobb of Eastern New Mexico University and Mary-Kate Sableski of the University of Dayton, who reviewed an earlier draft of this manuscript, and whose suggestions made this book a more valuable resource; and the many teachers who implemented the activities in this book and provided such excellent feedback. We also express our deepest appreciation and gratitude to our families, who support our work so enthusiastically.

CHAPTER ONE

Introduction

Learning to read is the most important accomplishment in a child's first few years of school. The ability to read well is a critical factor in later achievements in school and in life. Social and economic success in modern society is closely tied to an individual's level of literacy attainment (Anderson, Hiebert, Scott, & Wilkinson, 1985). Teaching children to read, therefore, is the fundamental mission of elementary schools. Unfortunately, many children experience difficulties in the early stages of learning to read that become barriers to later reading and learning. Much recent research in education has focused on the prevention of early reading problems (National Reading Panel, 2000; Snow, Burns, & Griffin, 1998).

One area of beginning reading research that has garnered an enormous amount of attention in the professional literature is phonological awareness. This research has been called "a scientific success story" (Stanovich, 1987), because researchers established such a clear link between a theoretical process and practical application (Morais, Mousty, & Kolinsky, 1998).

What Is Phonological Awareness?

Phonological awareness is the conscious sensitivity to the sound structure of language. It is the awareness that language is made up of various units of sound. Phonological awareness can also be thought of as an individual's capacity to attend to and reflect on the phonological components of spoken language, separate from meaning. Phonological awareness includes the abilities to detect, isolate, manipulate, blend, or segment units of sounds within the speech flow (Ehri, 1989). These metalinguistic abilities are essential for learning to read an alphabetic system of print such as English (Adams, 2001; Blachman, 1994, 2000; McBride-Chang, 1995; Stahl & Murray, 1994).

Speech is a complex phenomenon that includes movement, vibration, and air to make a large range of sounds. These sounds overlap during speech. As children learn to speak they learn to produce individual sounds, but the focus of their learning is on larger chunks of sound—words. Words are composed of other smaller linguistic units, called phonemes, syllables, onsets, and rimes. Syllables are combinations of phonemes that include a vowel or vowel-like speech sound. The onset of a syllable is any sound or sounds that come before the vowel (the *st* in *stop*);

> " Understanding the basic alphabetic principle requires an awareness that spoken language can be analyzed into strings of separable words, and words, in turn, into syllables and phonemes within syllables. "
>
> —Snow, Burns, & Griffin (1998, p. 15)

Definitions

Phonological Awareness— The awareness that spoken language can be broken into smaller units such as words, syllables, onsets and rimes, and phonemes.

Phoneme— The smallest unit of sound in spoken language.

Phonemic Awareness— The ability to reflect on and manipulate the smallest units of sound in language: phonemes.

Onset— In any syllable, the onset is the part of the syllable that precedes the vowel. In *meet,* the onset is /m/.

Rime— In any syllable, the rime includes all the sounds from the vowel to the end of the syllable. In *meet,* the rime is /eet/.

Syllable— Units of speech that consist of at least a vowel, but usually other sound(s) before and/or after the vowel, as well (e.g., *bat, sis-ter, mo-tor-cy-cle*).

the rime includes the vowel and any sounds that come after the vowel (the *op* in *stop*). Phonemes are the smallest units of sound in speech (for example, *ship* has three phonemes: /sh/, /i/, and /p/). These smaller linguistic units—syllables, onsets, rimes, and phonemes—are thoroughly embedded within the speech flow, which makes them difficult to detect and isolate. Isolating these linguistic units enables a reader to make connections between phonemes (sounds) and graphemes (letters). Developing an awareness of the individual phonemes in words is essential if a child is to understand the alphabetic nature of our written language (Ehri, 1998; Ehri & Soffer, 1999).

Why Is Phonological Awareness Important?

Numerous studies have demonstrated the importance of phonological awareness as the foundation for skilled decoding and, therefore, for fluent reading (e.g., Ball & Blachman, 1991; Cornwall, 1992; Lenchner, Gerber, & Routh, 1990; Liberman & Shankweiler, 1985; O'Connor, Notari-Syverson, & Vadasy, 1998; Pratt & Brady, 1988; Stanovich, 1986a; Wagner & Torgesen, 1987). The understanding that sounds in speech can be broken apart and blended together is necessary to make connections between speech and print. Without the ability to think about the individual sounds in words, matching sounds to letters and decoding words becomes extremely difficult. To benefit from phonics instruction, in which children are taught to make these letter-sound connections, a child must first have a fundamental level of phonological awareness.

Performance on phonological awareness tasks has been shown to be an excellent predictor of later reading ability or disability. That is, children who perform well on phonological awareness tasks are likely to become good readers, but children who perform poorly on phonological awareness tasks will likely become poor readers (Alegria & Morais, 1991; Badian, 1994; Blachman, 1991, 2000; Brady, 1997; Catts, 1991; Juel, Griffith, & Gough, 1986; Liberman & Shankweiler, 1991; Mann, 1986, 1991, 1993; Perfetti, 1991; Perfetti, Beck, Bell, & Hughes, 1987; Stanovich, 1986b, 1992; Vellutino & Scanlon, 1987; Wagner & Torgesen, 1987). In fact, it is estimated that more than 90 percent of children with significant reading problems have a core deficit in phonological processing (Blachman, 1995). This direct link between phonological awareness and later reading ability has generated much attention among reading researchers.

> "... teaching children to manipulate the sounds in words helps them learn to read."
>
> National Reading Panel (2000)

Phonological Awareness Research

Phonological awareness gained considerable attention in educational research during the 1980s and 1990s (see Blachman, 1994, 2000; Bus & van Ijzendoorn, 1999; and National Reading Panel, 2000, for reviews of this research). The primary attraction to this area of reading research was the repeated positive results in studies of phonological awareness interventions. Over the years, educational research has identified many reliable predictors of later reading performance (e.g., socioeconomic status, mother's education), but phonological awareness is one of the few factors that teachers are able to influence significantly. The numerous studies of phonological awareness have expanded the knowledge base in this area. A synthesis of this research yields several important generalizations:

- **Phonological awareness is directly related to reading ability**. That is, good readers typically have strong phonological awareness, and poor readers typically have weak phonological awareness.
- **Phonological awareness is a reliable predictor of later reading ability.** Teachers can assess children's phonological awareness in kindergarten and predict with a high degree of certainty which students, without targeted intervention, will be good or poor readers in fourth grade.
- **Although the relationship is reciprocal, phonological awareness precedes skilled decoding.** Decoding instruction helps a reader become better at both decoding and phonological awareness, but without some degree of phonological awareness development, skilled decoding is unlikely to develop at all. In fact, phonological awareness instruction that incorporates work with sounds *and* letters is more effective than instruction with only sounds.
- **Deficits in phonological awareness are usually associated with deficits in reading.** Most children who are diagnosed with significant reading problems demonstrate a core deficit in phonological processing.
- **Early language experiences play an important role in the development of phonological awareness.** The kinds of home and preschool experiences a child has can have a substantial influence on the child's phonological development. Children with a rich background of language experiences are much more likely to enter school with an awareness of the sound structure of language. In fact, a child's vocabulary size and phonological awareness development are linked.
- **Early intervention can promote the development of phonological awareness.** Intervention studies in preschool, kindergarten, and first grade have demonstrated over and over that direct teaching of phonological skills results in improvements in phonological awareness.
- **Improvements in phonological awareness can and usually do result in improvements in reading ability**. The most compelling finding from phonological awareness research is that improving phonological awareness usually improves reading ability. Children with strong phonological awareness typically benefit readily from phonics instruction. They are able to translate their understanding of speech sounds into letter-sound knowledge and decoding skill.

With poor phonological awareness, a child is unlikely to benefit from phonics instruction and, therefore, unlikely to become skilled at decoding words. Without the ability to quickly and accurately decode words, a child is extremely unlikely to become a fluent reader. Without the ability to read text fluently, a child is extremely unlikely to understand what she is reading. Although many other influences on comprehension exist, the connection between phonological awareness and reading comprehension is clear (see Figure 1.1).

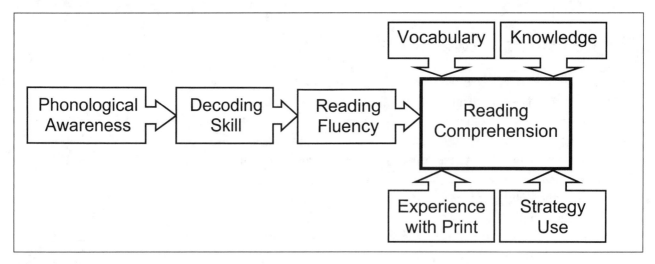

FIGURE 1.1   The influence of phonological awareness on reading comprehension.

Although a deficit in phonological processing is considered an identifying characteristic of dyslexia, such deficits alone cannot be considered sufficient evidence for diagnosis. Researchers have identified phonological awareness deficits as one of a set of problems that are extremely common among individuals with dyslexia, but other difficulties may be just as prevalent. In particular, deficits in naming speed ability have been found to be present in a large percentage of individuals with dyslexia (Badian, 1997; Wolf, 1997). Some researchers characterize these deficits as representative of a more global deficit in automization, or a difficulty in developing any novel skill to a level of automaticity (Fawcett & Nicholson, 1994). For purposes of clarity, this book will focus on the assessment and instruction of phonological skills and the role of these skills in the reading process.

Phonological Awareness Development

Although children come from a wide variety of backgrounds, initial reading instruction in schools is essentially the same for all children. Adams (1990) emphasized the importance of early reading and language experiences to the development of phonological awareness and reading skill. Adams evinced that many children come to school at a significant disadvantage due to severely limited early experiences with print. The development of phonological awareness requires experience with language activities, many of them informal and game-like, that promote linguistic awareness. Children who have been provided with a wide range of language and reading experiences may independently develop some level of phonological awareness.

Teachers can take an active role in developing their students' phonological awareness. Yopp (1992) promotes the use of activities that "facilitate children's ability to perceive that their speech is made up of a series of sounds" (p. 699). The emphasis should be placed on activities that focus on the sounds in spoken language. Specifically, Yopp suggested the use of activities such as sound matching, sound blending, sound addition, and sound segmentation. She also suggested that activities should be group-based and should encourage children's curiosity about language.

MacLean, Bryant, and Bradley (1987) tested the theory that children learn to analyze the component sounds in words through common linguistic routines, particu-

Is it ever too late to develop phonological awareness?

No! This answer is illustrated by the experience of one of our college students, a 23-year-old named Mac. Mac had reached college despite a significant reading disability. He had learned to read by memorizing words by sight and using context to guess words he did not know. He requested help when he began experiencing difficulty in reading the texts in his major—the first books he had ever cared about understanding. Initial assessments revealed that Mac could not decode even the simplest nonsense words (e.g., "ip"). Because he did not recognize them as words he had seen before, he had no idea how to figure them out. When prompted to "just sound it out," Mac responded, "What do you mean 'sound it out'? People have told me that before, but I never knew what they meant."

How did he get this far without learning how to sound out words? Well, Mac had experienced a terrible accident when he was only two years old. He had been electrocuted, which put him into a coma for six months. When he emerged from the coma, he did not speak again until he was seven years old. We know that children develop most of their phonological skills during the first six or seven years of their lives, and this explained much of Mac's difficulty. The rest of the problem occurred when Mac's teachers recognized his difficulty with phonics instruction. When they noticed he couldn't "do" phonics, they decided to do what most teachers at the time would have done—teach him sight words. Thus, Mac's underlying difficulty was never addressed.

Once he sought help for his reading difficulties in college, Mac's progress was astonishing. We began by working at the most fundamental levels of segmenting sentences into words and words into syllables. Very quickly, we moved to onsets and rimes and, finally, to phonemes. We matched sounds to letters and practiced blending phonemes together. In less than eighteen months of weekly tutoring sessions, Mac improved from not being able to decode "ip" to being able to decode any real word or nonsense word presented. Addressing Mac's underlying deficit in phonological awareness had erased his reading difficulties.

larly through nursery rhymes. The awareness that two words rhyme requires some awareness of the component sounds. MacLean et al. conducted a longitudinal study in which three-year-old children were assessed to determine their knowledge of nursery rhymes and their phonological skills. A strong direct correlation was detected and remained significant when differences in IQ and socioeconomic status were controlled.

Because phonological awareness is derived from speech information, some children develop a high degree of phonological awareness without any formal instruction (Kamhi & Catts, 1989). Such children, however, have typically had a variety of experiences with nonreading language play (Adams, 1990). Because such variations in phonological awareness may be found within a limited population of children, it is important to consider the different levels of phonological awareness and the implications of these levels for reading instruction.

Phonological Skills and Developmental Levels

Several skills that are commonly associated with beginning reading instruction help children develop phonological awareness. Typically, the first real phonological skill that children master is rhyming. Very young children may also master skills such as phoneme detection and sound matching with little instruction. More advanced phonological skills such as phoneme deletion, blending, and segmentation pose problems for many emergent readers. Most instruction designed to increase phonological awareness emphasizes these difficult skills (activities designed to enhance these skills are described in detail later in this book).

Levels of phonological awareness development are associated with the different phonological components of spoken language, including words, syllables, onsets and rimes, and phonemes (Blachman, 1991). Children tend to begin developing each level in sequence, but there is significant overlap among the levels. Effective assessment and instruction should address the various levels of phonological awareness development.

Phonological awareness is an "umbrella" term that encompasses a variety of metalinguistic skills and developmental levels (see Figure 1.2). Chapters 4 through 7 provide a more detailed explanation of each of the developmental levels of phonological awareness: word, syllable, onset-rime, and phoneme. The terms *phonological awareness* and *phonemic awareness* are used interchangeably—but incorrectly—by some educators. Phonemic awareness refers specifically to phonological awareness at the phoneme level, or the ability to detect, match, blend, segment, or otherwise manipulate individual sounds in words. Phonemic awareness is the level of phonological awareness necessary for skilled decoding (Adams, 2001; Chard, Simmons, & Kame'enui, 1998), because the capacity to attend to and manipulate sounds is necessary to use those sounds in concert with letters.

Although children must ultimately develop phonemic awareness to become skilled decoders, each level of phonological awareness helps children develop their facility

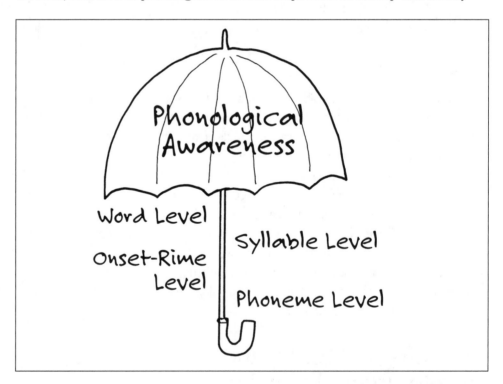

FIGURE 1.2 Developmental levels of phonological awareness.
Source: From "Preventing Reading Failure: Phonological Awareness Assessment and Instruction" by H. B. Lane, Paige C. Pullen, M. R. Eisele, and L. Jordan (2002). *Preventing School Failure, 46(2)*. Reprinted with permission of the Dwight Reid Education Foundation. Heldref Publications, 1319 18th Street, Washington, DC 20036-1802.

with sounds. The ability to manipulate words, syllables, onsets, and rimes, typically precedes the ability to manipulate phonemes. In Table 1.1, the most important phonological skills are described. The following chapters provide a variety of methods for assessing and developing these skills at each level of phonological awareness.

TABLE 1.1 **Common Phonological Awareness Skills**

SKILL/DESCRIPTION	EXAMPLE			
	Word Level	Syllable	Onset-Rime	Phoneme
Recognizing Rhyme				
Given a pair of words, the child determines if they rhyme.			*"Do these words rhyme? Hat, Sat"*	
Generating Rhyme				
Given a word, the child analyzes a word and thinks of a word with the same rime pattern.			*"Can you tell me a word that rhymes with 'car'?"*	
Matching Rhyme				
Given a list of words, the child identifies which words rhyme.			*"Which of these words rhyme? Tan, Fan, Sun"*	
Phoneme Detection				
Given a target sound, the child can determine if that sound is in the word. Detecting initial sounds is easier than final or medial sounds.				*"Tell me if you hear the /t/ in this word— Tub? Boat? Zoo?"*
Blending				
Given a word segmented into various sound units, the child can blend the sounds together to make the whole word.	*"I'm going to say a word in two parts* [pause between syllables]. You put the parts together to make a bigger word. Say "rain-bow." Child says, *"rainbow."*	*You put the parts together to make the whole word. Ready? Flow-er."* The child says, "flower."	At the onset-rime level, pause between the onset and rime (*b-oat*)	or at the phoneme level (*f-r-o-g*).
Segmenting				
This skill is the exact opposite of blending; given a whole word, the child can break the word into smaller chunks.	*"Can you break the word rainbow into two smaller words?"* [rain-bow]	*"Let's count the parts of the word tractor?"* [trac-tor]	*"Can you break the word rainbow into two smaller words?"* [rain-bow]	*"Can you say the word ship sound-by-sound?"* [sh-i-p]
Deletion (Elision)				
Given a whole word, the child can remove one unit of sound from the word.	*"Say sunshine."* [sunshine] *"Now say sunshine without saying sun"* [shine]	*"Say wonder."* [wonder] *"Now say wonder without saying won."* [der]	*"Say street."* [street] *"Now say street without saying s/tr/."* [eat]	*"Say meet."* [meet] *"Now say meet without saying /t/."* [me]

CHAPTER TWO

Assessing Phonological Awareness

Teachers are faced with the formidable challenge of determining which children have weaknesses in phonological awareness and, therefore, which children are likely to develop reading problems. Numerous methods for assessing phonological awareness have been developed. The choice of method to be used should be based on the purposes of assessment, the number of children to be assessed, the amount of existing information about these children, and the amount of time available.

The most reliable and informative method of assessing phonological awareness is in-depth, individual testing. Other methods have been developed, however, that are quick and easy to administer and that have adequate reliability for most purposes. Yopp (1988) investigated some of the most commonly used measures of phonological awareness and determined that the reliability and validity of measurement tasks was greatest when a combination of measures was used.

Perhaps the most important factor to consider when selecting any assessment measure is the purpose of the assessment. The three most common purposes for phonological awareness assessment are (1) *screening* groups of children to determine who is likely to experience difficulty, (2) *diagnosis* of specific phonological difficulties, and (3) *progress monitoring* to indicate which children are responding to a particular treatment. It is important to identify the purpose of phonological awareness assessment before selecting a specific instrument. The following sections outline assessment materials and methods that are useful for each of these three common purposes.

Screening

Group assessment of phonological awareness should be used for purposes of screening, not for diagnosis. Several methods for group screening of phonological skills have been developed. For example, the *Test of Phonological Awareness* (*TOPA*) is a standardized test that has been demonstrated to be an effective group-administered screening tool (Torgesen, Wagner, Bryant, & Pearson, 1992). The *TOPA*, which was designed for use with children in kindergarten and early elementary grades, requires students to identify sounds that are the same and different. The test is simple to administer in a group setting, yet sophisticated enough to detect individual differences in phonological awareness. Such a measure can be used to identify which children a teacher should target for further assessment and, possibly, intervention. *Phonological Awareness Literacy Screening* (*PALS*) provides another simple screening tool to identify children in need of phonological awareness intervention. There are three versions of *PALS*: Pre-kindergarten (Invernizzi, Sullivan, & Meier, 2001), Kindergarten (Invernizzi, Meier, Swank, & Juel, 1998), and First through Third Grades (Invernizzi & Meier, 2001). *PALS* measures a child's rhyming abilities and sound awareness. In addition to these phonological skills, alphabet knowledge, letter sound knowledge, concept of word, and word recognition are also assessed.

Adams (1990) describes reading and spelling as integrally related skills. Reading requires a child to translate written symbols (letters) into phonological representations (sounds) and to blend those sounds to form words. This process is also known as decoding. Spelling requires a child to translate segmented speech into sounds and to translate those spoken sounds into written symbols. This process is also known as encoding. A child who is unfamiliar with the spelling of a word may attempt to write that word based on limited knowledge about sound-symbol relationships. These efforts are known as invented spellings.

Invented spellings can be useful as a tool for phonemic awareness screening and for monitoring progress (Ehri, 1989; Tangel & Blachman, 1995; Treiman & Bourassa, 2000). Children's attempts to spell unfamiliar words demonstrate a great deal about their understanding of the sound structure of words (Brady, 1997). Mann, Tobin, and Wilson (1987) studied the use of invented spellings of kindergarten children as a measure of phonological awareness and as a predictor of reading ability. They concluded from this experiment that invented spelling performance in kindergarten may be used to predict first-grade reading ability. Children who produce a higher proportion of phonologically accurate preconventional spellings (e.g., *bot* for *boat, lade* for *lady*) tend to become better readers in the first grade.

Spelling an unfamiliar word requires the ability to segment the phonemes in the word. However, invented spellings also require understanding of the alphabetic principle. So, although strong performance on a test of invented spelling indicates strength in phonemic awareness, poor performance may indicate a weakness in phonemic awareness, a weakness in letter-sound knowledge, or a combination of these problems. Invented spelling measures should, therefore, be used only as a screening device to identify students in need of further assessment.

Several methods for scoring a child's invented spellings have been developed (see for example, Clay 1993; Invernizzi & Meier, 2001; Lane, Pullen, Eisele, & Jordan, 2002; Mann et al., 1987; Morris & Perney, 1984). In these scoring methods, points are awarded on the basis of a spelling's phonological accuracy. Children in the early stages of reading and spelling development might produce any of a wide range of spelling attempts. For example, in an attempt to spell an unfamiliar word, a child may produce a scribble, a random letter string, one or two correctly represented phonemes, or even a phonologically accurate spelling. Each of these attempts represents important information about that child's phonological knowledge and can help the teacher select appropriate skills to emphasize for instruction.

A sample test of invented spelling is provided in the Appendix, but teachers can easily devise their own tests. To evaluate children's phonological awareness using invented spellings, first choose ten to twenty words that provide a broad representation of target phonemes. Choose words that students are unlikely to be able to spell or recognize by sight. Separate tests can be administered using words and nonwords to ensure that spellings represent phonological knowledge rather than sight word knowledge.

When using nonwords, it is important to select words that use combinations of sounds that are plausible in the English language (e.g., *dup, neft,* or *slinch,* but not *dfe* or *tgazm*).

To administer an assessment of invented spellings, call out words to students and ask that they spell the words "just like they sound." To judge the quality of the invented spellings, consider each spelling's phonological accuracy. That is, is each sound in the word represented by a letter or combination of letters that can make that sound in the English language? Assign points to spellings based on the following scale:

- 0 points—no sounds in the word are represented by letters that can make that sound
- 1/2 point—if the word is represented by one or more phonemes other than the first
- 1 point—represented by the correct first phoneme
- 2 points—represented with two accurate phonemes, including the first
- 3 points—represented by the first correct phoneme and at least two additional correct phonemes, but not phonologically accurate
- 4 points—spelled with phonological accuracy (i.e., each sound in the word is represented by a letter that can make that sound)

See Figure 2.1 for examples of spellings at each level of scoring. The identification and appropriate representation of the initial phoneme in a word is heavily weighted in this scale. Typically, the initial phoneme is the easiest sound in a word for a child to detect and represent. Children who consistently fail to detect the correct initial sound in the word are more likely to have significant difficulty in their development of phonological skills.

Using this scale, scores that fall below an average of two points per word indicate poorly developed phonological awareness. Scores between an average of two and three points per word demonstrate developing phonological awareness and should be judged according to expectations for the student's age. In most cases, scores that average higher than three points per word indicate an understanding of basic phonological

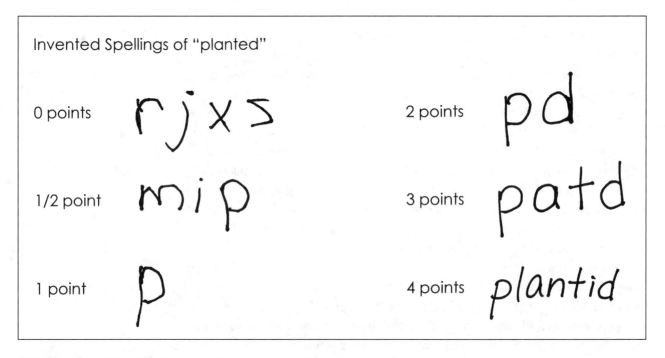

FIGURE 2.1 Examples of scores for invented spellings

concepts. In general, scores below an average of three points per word indicate a need for further individualized assessment.

This measure of invented spelling was administered with more than 2,000 children in kindergarten, first grade, and second grade, and scored using the described procedures (interscorer reliability > .97). Table 2.1 provides the percentiles for scores at each point of administration.

Diagnosis

Individual assessments are particularly useful to collect the kind of information about a child's phonological knowledge that is necessary to design effective instructional interventions. The assessment method can be informal, criterion-referenced, or norm-referenced. Clearly, the most direct informal method of measuring a child's phonological awareness is to observe the child's ability to perform tasks that require the use of phonological awareness. A variety of skill areas have been examined to identify phonological skills; these include rhyme detection and production, sound matching, phonemic oddity detection, deletion, segmentation, and blending.

Observation of phonological skills may take place during reading or language games, or the teacher may ask the student to perform specific phonological tasks. For example, to assess blending skills the teacher may ask the student to identify what word a given set of phonemes makes (e.g., "What word do these sounds make: /s/, /t/, /e/, /p/?"). To assess segmentation skills, the teacher may ask the student to say a word "sound by sound" (e.g., "Say 'cat' one sound at a time."). Performance on such tasks provides the teacher with significant information about the level of phonological skill a student possesses.

For more systematic assessment, a variety of simple tools are available. For example, the *Yopp-Singer Test of Phoneme Segmentation* is an individually administered assessment that requires students to segment two- and three-phoneme words. The *Rosner Test of Auditory Analysis* is an elision task in which children are asked

| | SPRING OF | FALL OF | SPRING OF | FALL OF |
PERCENTILE	KINDERGARTEN	1ST GRADE	1ST GRADE	2ND GRADE
90th	31.0	34.1	40.0	40.0
80th	28.0	31.5	38.0	39.0
70th	24.5	29.5	36.0	38.0
60th	22.5	27.5	35.0	36.5
50th	19.5	25.5	32.5	35.0
40th	16.5	23.5	29.5	33.5
30th	10.0	21.5	28.0	31.5
20th	6.0	18.3	24.0	29.5
10th	1.0	11.5	16.5	26.5

TABLE 2.1 Percentile ranks for invented spelling scores.

to delete portions of words. These measures are quick and easy to administer, yet they provide insight into a child's development in specific phonological processes.

In the Appendix, we provide several forms for use in assessing phonological awareness at each developmental level. These instruments allow for a quick, but comprehensive, diagnosis of phonological difficulties. The teacher asks the student to perform a series of phonological tasks at the word, syllable, onset-rime, and phoneme levels. These tasks include many of the critical phonological skills. A more thorough explanation of the purposes and methods for the assessments for each level of phonological awareness may be found in Chapters 4 through 7.

The *Lindamood Auditory Conceptualization Test* (*LAC;* Lindamood & Lindamood, 1979) provides a formal, standardized method for measuring phonological awareness. Calfee, Lindamood, and Lindamood (1973) studied the effectiveness and the predictive validity (for reading and spelling performance) of the *LAC* with students in kindergarten through twelfth grade. They concluded that the *LAC* is an effective measure of phonological awareness and that it is highly predictive of word reading and spelling performance through high school.

The *Comprehensive Test of Phonological Processing* (*CTOPP;* Wagner, Torgesen, & Rashotte, 1999) is a diagnostic tool that measures several critical phonological processing skills. In addition to phonological awareness, this assessment measures phonological memory and rapid naming. Phonological memory refers to the ability to code information phonologically for temporary storage in working or short-term memory. In the context of the *CTOPP,* rapid naming refers to efficient retrieval of phonological information from long-term memory and the ability to execute a sequence of operations automatically. Each of these phonological processes is important in reading, and the test provides a profile from which a teacher can plan effective instruction. Norms for the *CTOPP* are available from kindergarten to college.

The *Developmental Spelling Analysis* (*DSA;* Ganske, 2000) provides a standardized screening inventory and a series of feature inventories that allow for both screening and diagnosis of spelling difficulties. The initial stages of spelling development, as outlined by Ganske, rely heavily on a child's phonemic awareness and understanding of the alphabetic principle. Teachers can use these measures to determine where to focus instruction.

Progress Monitoring

Effective tools are essential to monitor the progress of children who are struggling in the development of phonological awareness. Once problems have been identified and intervention begun, periodic measures of progress allow the teacher to determine whether the intervention is working or if changes are warranted. Although teacher observation is invaluable for keeping track of growth for most children, monitoring the progress of children at risk for reading failure requires more precision.

Several of the measures described as tools for diagnosis may also be used for progress monitoring purposes. For example, the *CTOPP* may be used both before and after an intervention to determine the effectiveness of the intervention. The *DSA* can be used to measure growth from one stage of spelling to the next. The *Sound Beginning* instruments found in the Appendix may be used two or three times during the year to measure growth at each level of phonological awareness.

Dynamic Indicators of Basic Early Literacy Skills (*DIBELS*) is designed specifically for monitoring children's progress throughout the school year. *DIBELS* includes two measures of Phonological Awareness: Initial Sounds Fluency (ISF), which assesses a child's ability to identify and produce the initial sound of an orally presented word, and Phonemic Segmentation Fluency (PSF), which assesses a child's ability to segment the sounds within a three- or four-phoneme word (Kaminski & Good, 1996). The tests are timed, and measure a student's fluency or automaticity with each skill. These measures are quick and easy to administer and provide an excellent way to monitor progress during kindergarten and first grade, the most critical period of phonological awareness development. The *DIBELS* measure may also be used for initial screening purposes.

Selecting Appropriate Assessments

Clearly, the purpose for which assessment data will be used is the most important factor to consider when selecting methods and materials for phonological awareness assessment. It is also important to consider the reliability and validity of particular measures. Researchers at the University of Oregon have developed a clearinghouse for information about reading assessments. For each assessment, they have outlined the specific utility of the measure for various purposes. This web-based resource (http://idea.uoregon.edu/assessment/) allows school districts and individual teachers access to valuable information about assessment instruments they may be considering for use in their schools and classrooms.

CHAPTER THREE

Designing Instruction to Develop Phonological Awareness

If a child's level of phonological awareness is predictive of that child's reading ability, then can poor phonological awareness be remediated? If so, will remediation result in improved reading ability? The answers to these questions illustrate why phonological awareness research is considered a scientific success story (Stanovich, 1987). The National Reading Panel's (2000) meta-analysis of phonological awareness research indicates unequivocally that instruction can improve phonemic awareness and that these improvements lead to improvements in reading.

The work of Elkonin (1963), a Russian psychologist, was perhaps the earliest documented instruction that dealt specifically with phonological awareness. Elkonin speculated that children must be able to hear, distinguish, and analyze the separate sounds in words to be able to learn to read. Subsequently, he created a teaching method that would allow for the development of these skills. Elkonin provided counters and pictures of objects with squares drawn beneath each picture representing the number of separate sounds in the word. The child was asked to segment the phonemes in the word while placing one counter in a square for each sound. This instruction resulted in increased abilities in phonemic segmentation and increased decoding skills. Methods similar to Elkonin's have been used successfully in a number of subsequent studies by other researchers. Elkonin boxes are described in detail in chapter 7.

Many phonological awareness studies have emphasized the various aspects of instruction. Some researchers have examined the methods of or approaches to instruction. Others have concentrated on the skills addressed within instructional programs. Still others have investigated the levels of phonological awareness addressed. The findings from all of these studies can inform the design of effective phonological awareness instruction.

Torgesen, Morgan, and Davis (1992) compared the effects on the development of phonological awareness skills and on word learning of phonological awareness programs that emphasized blending only or a combination of blending and segmentation. They concluded that phonological awareness instruction that includes both types of tasks provides a richer awareness of the phonological structure of words. In a similar study, O'Connor, Jenkins, Leicester, and Slocum (1993) found that children taught one type of phonological skill did not automatically generalize to other skills. Haskell, Foorman, and Swank (1992) examined whether the whole-word level, the onset-rime level, or the phoneme level of phonological awareness is more effective for instruction. They concluded that onset-rime instruction may foster flexibility in applications of spelling patterns, while phoneme instruction is more beneficial for reading words with regular spellings.

Designing Effective Instruction

Just as assessing phonological awareness is best accomplished by having students perform tasks that demonstrate phonological skills, developing phonological awareness requires practicing phonological skills. Phonological awareness instruction should be designed to help children understand the fundamental notion that words can be conceived as sequences of phonemes (Adams, 2001; Chard & Osborne, 1999; Smith, Simmons, & Kame'enui, 1998).

Implicit or explicit instruction? For most children, phonological awareness instruction can be easily incorporated within the context of meaningful reading or writing. Some children, however, require more extensive practice with skills (Chard & Dickson, 1999; Smith et al., 1998). For children who are struggling, explicitly teaching them to apply their phonological skills is more effective than implicit instruction (Cunningham, 1990). Explicit instruction is clear and without ambiguity. In well-designed and implemented explicit instruction, children know exactly what they are supposed to learn and they know when they have learned it.

Appropriate explicit instruction benefits all students (Fielding-Barnsley, 1997), but students who have very low levels of reading skill benefit most from explicit instruction in phonological skills paired with explicit instruction in how to apply those skills in a meaningful context (Lane, 1994). Adams (2001) explains that the goal of explicit instruction is to help children focus their attention on important points, because "that which one learns depends on that to which one attends" (p. 75). Without explicit teaching, many children do not develop sufficient phonological skills, and others do not understand how to apply the skills they do have.

The degree to which phonological awareness instruction is explicit should depend on student characteristics and curricular demands (Mercer, Lane, Jordan, Allsopp, & Eisele, 1996). For students with insufficient background knowledge and experiences, explicit instruction is necessary. For students with a rich background in language and much experience with language play, a more implicit, discovery-oriented approach may suffice. Mastering specific phonological skills may require explicit instruction, but the degree to which the application of these skills must be taught will vary from student to student. The complex and abstract nature of the sounds in our language makes explicit phonological awareness instruction particularly important. As Adams (2001) points out, during normal speaking and listening, one's attention is focused on the meaning of the message, not on the phonemes in the words. Explicit teaching may be required to draw a child's attention to the abstract and sometimes difficult-to-detect sounds in words.

Time and grouping arrangements. Instruction in phonological skills can be conducted as formal, structured lessons, as an integrated part of ongoing reading instruction, or as fun activities throughout the school day (Smith et al., 1998). Instruction may be individualized, small-group, or whole-class.

The National Reading Panel (2000), in their meta-analysis of phonological awareness research, concluded that more instruction is not necessarily better. The amount of instruction provided should be dictated by the needs of children, but in general, interventions that lasted approximately five to eighteen cumulative hours demonstrated the best results. They also concluded that small-group instruction is more effective for most children than either whole-class or one-on-one instruction. For children with typically developing phonological awareness, ten to fifteen minutes of instruction two or three days per week for a few months during kindergarten may be sufficient. For students who have significant weaknesses in phonological awareness, fifteen to twenty-five minutes of small-group or even one-on-one instruction each day throughout kindergarten and first grade may be necessary to promote adequate growth.

Methods of instruction. Studies of phonological awareness intervention have demonstrated that many forms of instruction can be effective. However, several properties of instruction lead to better results. For example, phonemic awareness instruction that includes letters is more effective than instruction that does not include letters (Hatcher, Hulme, & Ellis, 1994; Iversen & Tunmer, 1993; National Reading Panel, 2000; Torgesen, Wagner, & Rashotte, 1997). Phoneme blending instruction with letters helps children learn to decode words (Kroese, Hynd, Knight, Hall, & Hiemenz, 2000; Lane, Pullen, & Hudson, 2003; Pullen, 2000; Wesseling & Reitsma, 2000); segmenting phonemes with letters helps children learn to spell words (Kroese et al., 2000; Hatcher & Hulme, 1999; Lane et al., 2003; Treiman & Bourassa, 2000).

Phonological awareness instruction should be engaging. Many programs designed to develop phonological awareness emphasize the use of games. Making learning fun can keep children engaged in what might otherwise be an extremely challenging experience. Instruction in phonological awareness can also be formal or informal. For most children, informal language play that calls their attention to the phonological components of language may be sufficient. For some children, however, more directed lessons with built-in assessment may be necessary.

The most effective phonological awareness instruction . . .

- is explicit for children who are struggling.
- is conducted in small groups.
- occurs frequently, for short periods of time.
- focuses on one or two phonological skills.
- includes connections to letters.
- emphasizes phoneme blending and segmentation skills.
- provides opportunities for application of skills in connected text.
- is provided by teachers who are knowledgeable about the structure of language.

Phonological skills. Phonological awareness instruction can include a variety of skills. For example, children may be taught to categorize phonemes, blend onsets and rimes, generate rhymes, segment syllables, blend phonemes into words, or segment words into individual phonemes. Instruction might include one of these skills or all of them. All of these approaches can improve children's abilities in phonological awareness, but instruction that focuses on one or two skills is more effective than instruction that includes more skills (National Reading Panel, 2000).

Sources of instruction. The National Reading Panel (2000) also considered the source of phonological awareness instruction. In some of the studies reviewed, classroom teachers provided the instruction. In others, instruction was provided by researchers or specially trained individuals. In still other studies, instruction was provided via a computer. All forms of instruction yielded positive results, but the meta-analysis revealed that instruction from teachers and researchers was more effective than instruction from computers. For children who are struggling, is it also important to ensure that instruction is provided by someone with sufficient expertise to recognize and respond appropriately to individual differences.

Commercially Available Instructional Programs

Several commercial programs are designed to develop phonological awareness. For example, *Lindamood Phoneme Sequencing Program for Reading, Spelling, and Speech* (*LiPS*), formerly called *Auditory Discrimination in Depth* (Lindamood & Lindamood, 1975), is an intensive program for developing auditory conceptualization, as the program developers refer to what we now call phonological awareness. *LiPS* develops phonological awareness by drawing a child's attention to the motoric features of phoneme articulation through individual or small group instruction. Sounds are categorized according to where and how they are produced. Students learn, through Socratic questioning, to associate speech sounds with the specific part of the vocal anatomy that produces the sound (the sounds for *b* and *p,* for example, are called "lip poppers"). This level of attention to sound production heightens students' awareness of the sound itself. Students learn to manipulate colored blocks that represent individual phonemes and, eventually, to connect the sounds with letters.

Adams, Foorman, Lundberg, and Beeler (1998) developed a comprehensive program called *Phonemic Awareness in Young Children: A Classroom Curriculum* that provides a basis for assessment and instruction in phonological awareness. This program is an English translation and adaptation of a Danish program designed and tested by Lundberg, Frost, and Petersen (1988). The program includes a variety of language games, listening games, rhyming activities, and activities for developing students' understanding of sounds in words. Several instruments for assessing phonological awareness are included, as well.

Road to the Code (Blachman, Ball, Black, & Tangel, 2000) includes activities to move students from phonological awareness to letter knowledge. The core activity in *Road to the Code* is the "Say It-Move It," in which children learn to blend sounds together to form words. The program gradually moves into activities that encourage the application of these skills in writing and spelling. Implementation of *Road to the Code* has resulted in long-term benefits for struggling beginning readers (Blachman, Tangel, Ball, Black, & McGraw, 1999).

Ladders to Literacy: A Preschool Activity Book (Notari-Syverson, O'Connor, & Vadasy, 1998) and *Ladders to Literacy: A Kindergarten Activity Book* (O'Connor, Notari-Syverson, & Vadasy, 1998) are instructional materials to guide teachers in developing a variety of skills. These books provide early literacy activities in phonological awareness, as well as vocabulary development, letter names, and sounds. The unique feature of these books is the distinction made in each lesson about the amount of teacher support that should be provided and explanations about how and when to vary this support.

Another effective commercial program is *Phonological Awareness Training for Reading* (Torgesen & Bryant, 1994), which provides a simple method for group instruction in phonological awareness. This program uses Rocky Robot to teach students the concepts of phoneme segmentation and blending. The instruction in this program is designed to help students apply phonological skills during reading.

Computer-Assisted Instruction

Computer-assisted instruction is a viable alternative for developing phonological awareness (Barker & Torgesen, 1995; Reitsma & Wesseling, 1998; Torgesen & Barker, 1995; Wise, King, & Olson, 2000). Using appropriate software, children can learn phoneme identity, blending, and segmenting skills. In schools where personnel shortages prevent the necessary small-group or one-on-one instruction some children need, use of effective computer software can help children from falling too far behind.

Read, Write, and Type (Herron, Sabbag, & Rechis, 1995) is a computer-based program that incorporates the development of phonological skills into writing activities. As they type each letter on the computer keyboard, students hear an isolated phoneme. As they type combinations of letters, the phonemes are blended into words. For each phoneme, the students are guided through a set of motivating activities that emphasize phoneme detection, sound matching, and blending skills. As an added bonus, the program teaches keyboarding skills as it teaches phonological skills.

Daisy Quest and *Daisy's Castle* (Erikson, Foster, Foster, & Torgesen, 1992, 1993) are computer programs for the Macintosh. The games are motivating for children while providing opportunities to develop phonological awareness at each level. Research studies have found these software programs to be an effective way to stimulate phonological awareness in young children.

Several other software programs have become popular in schools as well. *Earobics* (Wasowicz, 1997, 1999) is a software program designed to develop phonemic awareness and letter-sound knowledge through engaging games. The *Waterford Early Reading Program* (Waterford Institute, 1993) is a comprehensive computer program for kindergarten. It provides activities in phonological awareness, concepts of print, letter names, and letter sounds. *Fast ForWord* (Merzenich, Tallal, Jenkins, & Miller, 1996) is an interactive program that stimulates children's phonological skills using acoustically modified speech sounds. The computer lengthens the pronunciation of speech sounds in ways that human speech cannot to make the sounds easier to detect for children who are struggling. The phonemes are then systematically shortened, so the child can gradually learn to detect sounds pronounced naturally. This acoustic training is provided in five twenty-minute sessions each day and requires teacher training. Each of these software programs has a distinct purpose and develops specific skills. Care should be taken to match the features of the program with the instructional needs of students.

Informal Methods of Instruction

Most activities in commercial programs such as those described can be incorporated informally within existing reading instruction. The activities in the following chapters are useful for practicing and developing phonological skills. The activities are sequenced by level, in an order that approximates the developmental sequence. However, it should be noted that the sequence and rate of skill development varies from child to child, and skills overlap during development. Many of the activities that are described in relation to one level may be readily modified to teach phonological awareness at one of the other levels. It should also be noted that all of these activities are *auditory* and *interactive* in nature—each activity requires the students, and often the teacher, to be engaged in active oral communication. Children do not develop phonological skills by doing independent written work.

Creating and Organizing a Picture Card File

In many of the activities in this book we refer to a picture card file, which is quite simple to make. We have found that the easiest way to create a picture card file is to locate colored pictures from graphics or clipart software, print those pictures on a colored printer and glue onto 3" × 5" unlined index cards.

The organization of the picture card file is the key to its utility. We recommend organizing the cards into three main categories: cards for rhyming games, cards for syllable games, and cards for phoneme games. For the syllable and phoneme cards, file them based on the number of syllables or phonemes in the word. You will then be ready to use the pictures for quick activities during transitions, or to select picture cards for various games such as those described in the following chapters.

Throughout the following chapters, there are two types of activities. All of the activities develop phonological awareness, but some of them use only sounds, and others incorporate letters. Those activities that incorporate letters are phonics activities and are designated with the following icon:

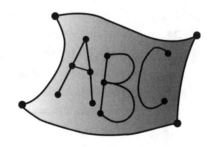

CHAPTER FOUR

The Word Level

The most fundamental level of phonological awareness is the word level. Awareness that the speech flow is a compilation of individual words is typically achieved at a very young age. Because humans pronounce words in an overlapping or co-articulated fashion, the speech flow does not have many actual breaks between words. Because words are the parts of the speech flow with the most readily identifiable meaning, we also use meaning to help us identify where one word ends and the next one begins. Therefore, oral language abilities and vocabulary development can play an important role in the development of phonological awareness.

Consider the challenge of listening to two people speak in a language you are only beginning to learn. Their speech is likely to sound amazingly fast and jumbled, because you have learned only a few words. Your ability to identify individual words in the speech flow depends heavily upon your knowledge of the meaning and pronunciation of words within that flow. When you hear one of the words you have learned, you may understand only that word, or you may miss it altogether because it is pronounced too quickly with other words around it. Your ability to attend to small parts of sound is inhibited by the speed of the speech flow.

As children learn individual words, they begin to notice when adults say those words in the flow of natural speech. Sometimes, however, children learn a new word that they have never heard said in isolation. For example, a baby may have only heard the word *bottle* pronounced in the context of the speech flow, never in isolation ("Let me get your bottle for you, sweetie." "Oops, you dropped your bottle on the floor!"). But one day, that baby utters "bah" or some other approximation of the word *bottle.* This utterance is evidence that the child has isolated *bottle,* a word of particular significance, from the stream of words around it. When a child utters a single word that he has only heard in combination with other words, he is demonstrating the word level of phonological awareness.

The linguistic play of young children, including rhyming and the generation of

Ms. Hayes and her kindergarten students are reciting Humpty Dumpty. This time, she asks each child to represent one word in the poem. As she goes around the circle pointing to individual students, they reply . . .

"Humpty," says Brett.
"Dumpty!" shouts Naomi.
"sat," Raheed calls out.

. . . and so forth, until they have recited the entire poem. As they get to the end, they begin again, and each child gets a new word. These children are learning what constitutes a word.

nonsense words, provides evidence of this early level of phonological awareness (Bradley, 1988). Such play should be encouraged when it occurs spontaneously. Most children, however, learn to play with words through interactions with adults, so the role of parents and preschool teachers in the development of word-level awareness is extremely important. Very few children have difficulty developing this level of phonological awareness, but word-level activities can enhance a child's conscious sensitivity to individual words in the speech flow.

Word Level Assessment

Assessment of phonological awareness at the word level can be accomplished by asking children to manipulate words in sentences or individual words within compound words. The following assessment uses two tasks to determine whether a student has developed phonological awareness at the word level. In the first task, Tapping Words, the teacher begins by modeling for the student how to say a sentence while tapping once for each word. A child who is struggling at this level might tap once for each syllable, tap randomly, or tap to the rhythm of speech in the sentence without attending to word boundaries. In the second task, Deleting Words, the teacher provides a compound word and then asks the child to say the compound word while removing one of the parts (e.g., "Say motorcycle. Now say motorcycle without saying motor."). Most children in mid-kindergarten or beyond are able to perform tasks such as these with minimal effort. Difficulty with these tasks could indicate a potentially significant problem with phonological awareness, auditory perception or processing, or perhaps, hearing acuity, and would warrant more in-depth evaluation. A blank version of this assessment form may be found in the Appendix.

Word Level Activities

Word level activities are designed to develop the student's sensitivity to individual words within the speech flow, and most of the activities are quite simple. This level of activity is most appropriate for children in preschool and kindergarten. Older children with severe language deficits may also have difficulty with and need practice at this level. The following pages contain suggested activities to develop phonological awareness at the word level.

ACTIVITIES
- ☐ Tapping Words
- ☐ Connecting Words
- ☐ Counting and Tallying Words
- ☐ Matching Words
- ☐ Adding Attributes
- ☐ Silly Sentence Switching
- ☐ Jumping Jingles
- ☐ Blending Words
- ☐ Add a Word
- ☐ Matchsticks

TARGET SKILLS
- ☐ Blending Words
- ☐ Segmenting Words
- ☐ Deleting Words
- ☐ Matching Words
- ☐ Adding Words
- ☐ Substituting Words

A Sound Beginning

Phonological Awareness Assessment

SKILL: Tapping Words

DIRECTIONS: Say words in bold to student. **In this word game, I want you to tap one time for every word you hear in my sentence. So, if I say, "*An apple is red,*" you tap like this."** [Model saying the sentence and tapping 4 times.] **Now you try.** Repeat with practice item and provide corrective feedback as needed. Do not provide corrective feedback on the test items.

PRACTICE ITEM: "The little frog is jumping."

TEST ITEMS:	ANSWER	(+/–)
1. Sue is my friend.	4 TAPS	+
2. My mother is calling me.	5 TAPS	+
3. The dog is chasing the kittens.	6 TAPS	+
4. The boy is running.	4 TAPS	+
5. She is wearing a purple jacket.	6 TAPS	–
	Word Tapping Score	**4/5**

SKILL: Deleting Words

PRACTICE ITEM: Say COWBOY. Now say COWBOY without saying BOY.

TEST ITEMS:	ANSWER	(+/–)
1. Say SAILBOAT. Now say SAILBOAT without saying SAIL.	BOAT	+
2. Say APPLESAUCE. Now say APPLESAUCE without saying SAUCE.	APPLE	+
3. Say SIDEWALK. Now say SIDEWALK without saying SIDE.	WALK	+
4. Say SUNSHINE. Now say SUNSHINE without saying SUN.	SHINE	+
5. Say CUPCAKE. Now say CUPCAKE without saying CAKE.	CUP	+
	Word Deletion Score	**5/5**
	Total Word Level Score	**9/10**

FIGURE 4.1 Sample word level phonological awareness assessments

Tapping Words

Target Skill

Segmenting words

Materials

Rhythm sticks

Sandpaper blocks

Other percussion instruments

Directions

Children tap out the words in a sentence with rhythm sticks. The teacher reads a sentence, the child repeats the sentence and taps once for each word. Begin with short sentences and gradually add words. Initially, sentences should contain only one-syllable words. For example, for "My dog is cute," the child taps the rhythm sticks four times. After the child is able to tap sentences with one-syllable words, add multi-syllable words, like "I have a soft puppy." As the task increases in difficulty, add the support needed so that the child is successful.

Variations: Use various percussion instruments to modify this activity. Other variations include clapping the words or tapping quietly on a table with one finger.

4.2 Connecting Words

Target Skill

Segmenting words

Materials

Linking cubes or linking chains (available through mathematics materials catalogs)

Connecting Words Activity Sheet (see Appendix)

Directions

Provide each student with a set of connecting cubes or chains. Read a sentence aloud. The child adds one cube for each word in a sentence. This activity can be implemented in small groups or with the whole class. Ask the children to hold up their cubes and quickly assess who may need additional support with word level awareness.

Variation: Provide children with a copy of the Connecting Words activity sheet (see Appendix). As you read the sentence aloud, the children will color one box for each word in the sentence. The children can then count the words in each sentence read.

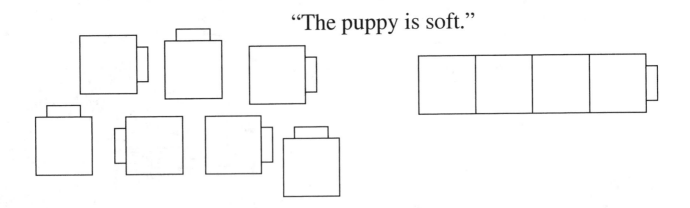

"The puppy is soft."

Counting and Tallying Words

Counting and tallying the number of words in a sentence requires a greater degree of cognitive engagement than tapping words. After children are able to tap words successfully, the following activities are appropriate.

Target Skill

Segmenting words

Materials

Construction paper

Sponge-tipped moistener stick (available from office supply stores and used to moisten envelopes)

Counters (e.g., beads, counting chips)

Small paper cups

Directions

ACTIVITY 1:

Provide each child with a sponge-tipped moistener stick filled with water and a large sheet of construction paper. As the teacher reads a sentence aloud, the child taps the moistener on his construction paper one time for each word. The child then counts the number of dots to determine the number of words in the sentence. The construction paper will dry and the dots will no longer be visible. You are ready for the next sentence.

ACTIVITY 2:

Provide each child with a cup and several beads. Read the sentence and ask the children to put one bead in the cup for each word.

Matching Words

Target skill

Matching words

Materials

Sentence pocket chart

Poems or nursery rhymes printed on sentence strips, two times
   (the second set of sentence strips should be cut apart, word by word)

Directions

Post a poem or rhyme that is familiar to the students. Give each student a word from the poem printed on the sentence strip. The class then recites the poem or nursery rhyme together while the teacher points to the words. After each stanza, ask the children to come up one at a time and match their word card to the word in the poem by placing the card in the pocket chart. (Tip: To prevent confusion when a word appears multiple times in the rhyme, print each sentence strip in a different color. The student word cards would be printed in the corresponding color.)

Variation 1: Instead of simply matching words, have all students with the words from the first stanza come to the front of the class and stand side-by-side in the correct order of the stanza. Allow each child to read his or her word in order. The child reading can step forward as he/she reads the word. Repeat the game for each stanza until all children have had the opportunity to participate.

Variation 2: Have children stand in a circle. Recite a poem or nursery rhyme, having each child in the circle say one word. For example, begin by reciting Jack Be Nimble all together. Then have one child begin by saying, "Jack," the next says, "be," the next "nimble," etc. until you have finished reciting the nursery rhyme. Repeat the rhyme, and the second time around the circle the students will each have a new word.

Sentence Strips

Mary had a little lamb.

Its fleece was white as snow.

Everywhere that Mary went,

the lamb was sure to go.

Student Word Cards

Mary	had	a
little	lamb	Its
fleece	was	white
as	snow	Everywhere
that	Mary	went
the	lamb	was
sure	to	go

Adding Attributes

Target Skill

Adding words

Materials

Attribute tiles

Stuffed animal, or various objects in classroom

Directions

Place an attribute tile on the overhead projector. Ask students to describe the tile beginning with one word. Then, the second child adds a different attribute. This sequence is continued until as many attributes as possible are named. Keep track of the number of attributes named. Instead of tiles, stuffed animals or other objects in the classroom may be used.

Variation: Ask children to add descriptive words that begin with the same sound (e.g., bear, brown bear, big brown bear, beautiful big brown bear).

How many words can you use to describe me?

Silly Sentence Switching

Target skill

Matching words

Directions

Children sit in a circle. Begin by stating a sentence such as "The red bike rolled down the road." Taking turns by moving around the circle, each child can change one word in the sentence. For example, the first child could change the sentence to "The blue bike rolled down the road." The next child could say, "The blue car rolled down the road." The next child would change one word in that sentence, "The blue car rolled up the road." (Note: The sentences that the children create do not need to make sense!)

Jumping Jingles

4.7

Target Skill

Segmenting words

Materials

Large floor lily pads (rubber matting such as a shower slip pad cut into lily pad shapes)

Jingles or nursery rhymes

Directions

Place the lily pads on the floor in a line, close enough together that the children can jump easily from one lily pad to another. Generate a list of popular commercial jingles or select common nursery rhymes. Begin with jingles that contain single syllable words only and move to sentences that include words with more than one syllable. Read a sentence one time through. Then read the sentence again, this time having the child jump from one lily pad to another for each word read.

Variations for more sophisticated levels of phonological awareness

Variation 1: Play the game in the same way; however, have students jump from lily pad to lily pad for each syllable in a multisyllable word for a syllable-level activity.

Variation 2: Play the game in the same way; however, have students jump from lily pad to lily pad for each phoneme in a word.

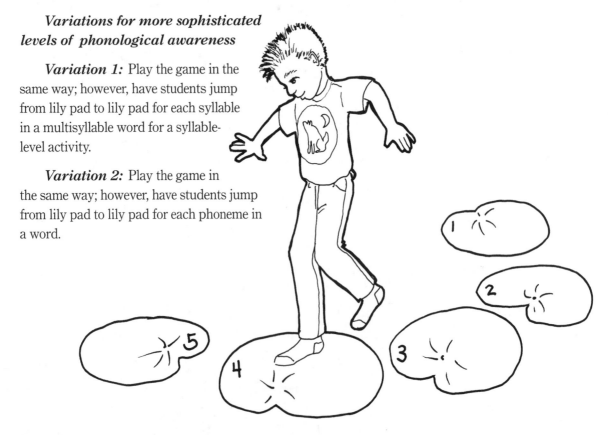

Blending Words

Target Skill

Blending words

Materials

List of familiar compound words (see Appendix)

Picture Cards

Directions

Two critical skills in phonological awareness are blending and segmenting at the phoneme level. However, children can begin to develop the skill of blending at the word level using compound words. Select pictures from your picture card file to illustrate common compound words. Say, "I'm going to say this word one part at a time. You put the parts together to make the whole word, *foot-ball*. What word?" Children respond, "Football."

Variation: After children become competent using picture cards, play the game in the same way without the picture cards as cues. It is helpful to use hand signals to guide the children in answering chorally. Hold one fist up as you call out the first word, then repeat with the other hand. Put your hands together when you want the children to respond.

4.9

Add a Word

Target Skills

Segmenting words

Materials

None

Directions

Select three children and assign each child a word to say in front of the class as they stand in a line. Together the children's words should form a simple sentence (e.g., "I like pizza."). Ask the class to think of a word they could add to the sentence to make it longer. Have a student represent the new word and stand in the appropriate place in line (e.g., "I like *cheese* pizza."). Then have students repeat their words to form the new sentence.

Some words may need helping words before they can be added, so help your children determine what is necessary to add a new word. For example, if a student wants to add pepperoni, you would need either a "with" or an "and" to form "I like cheese pizza with pepperoni" or I like cheese and pepperoni pizza." Ask the child who came up with the word *pepperoni* to select a classmate to represent the helping word. Challenge the children to make the sentence as long as possible. They may be able to make a sentence involving every child in the class! A kindergarten class created the following sentences.

- I like pizza.
- I like cheese pizza.
- I like cheese and pepperoni pizza.
- I like to eat cheese and pepperoni pizza.
- I like to eat cheese and pepperoni pizza at Leonardo's.
- I like to eat cheese and pepperoni pizza at Leonardo's with Lauren.
- I like to eat cheese and pepperoni pizza at Leonardo's with my friend Lauren.
- I like to eat cheese and pepperoni pizza at Leonardo's with my best friend Lauren.
- I like to eat cheese and pepperoni pizza on Saturday at Leonardo's with my best friend Lauren.
- I like to eat cheese and pepperoni pizza for lunch on Saturday at Leonardo's with my best friend Lauren.
- I like to eat cheese and pepperoni pizza for lunch on Saturday at Leonardo's with my best friend Lauren and Taylor.
- I like to eat cheese and pepperoni pizza for lunch on Saturday at Leonardo's with my best friend Lauren and her brother Taylor.
- I like to eat cheese and pepperoni pizza for lunch on Saturday at Leonardo's with my best friend Lauren and her little brother Taylor.

4.10

Matchsticks

Target Skills

Blending words

Materials

Picture cards

Tongue depressors

Directions

Select a variety of pairs of picture cards that, when combined, form compound words (e.g., a picture of a bird and a picture of a house to form *birdhouse*). Attach the pictures to tongue depressors. Provide each child with a "stick" (tongue depressor with picture attached). Call out "MATCHSTICKS" and the children will then search among their classmates for a matching stick. When each pair has been matched, have them say each word pictured and blend the two words to form the compound word.

Select compound words with component words that children will recognize readily. Here are some suggested compound words for this activity: catfish, sunflower, rainbow, football, birdhouse, pancake, ladybug, dragonfly, cupcake, armchair, pinball, raincoat, and keyboard.

CHAPTER FIVE

The Syllable Level

The syllable level is typically the first level of formal instruction in phonological awareness, because syllables are the most easily distinguishable units within words. The ability to segment syllables typically precedes the ability to segment phonemes (Liberman, Shankweiler, Fischer, & Carter, 1974). Most children acquire the ability to segment words into syllables with minimal instruction (Liberman, Shankweiler, & Liberman, 1989; Lundberg, 1988; Notari-Syverson et al., 1998). Activities such as clapping, tapping, and marching are often used to develop syllable awareness in preschool and kindergarten classrooms. Learning the term "syllable" is not important for children; learning the concept of syllables in words and learning how to manipulate them *is* important.

Each day, as the children in her first-grade class line up for lunch, Ms. Sprague encourages them to think about the sounds of language. Yesterday, she told them, "If you have two syllables in your first name, it's your turn to line up. Now, everybody who has one syllable, line up." And so on, until all the children were in line. Today, she asks them, "Who has three syllables in their last name? It's your turn to line up. . . ." Tomorrow, she will ask children to count the syllables in their first *and* last names combined. Ms. Sprague never misses an opportunity to get her children to think!

This level of phonological awareness is useful for initial instruction in detection, segmentation, blending, and manipulation of phonological components of language. Once students acquire these skills at the syllable level, acquisition at more sophisticated levels becomes somewhat easier. Unlike words, most syllables do not have meanings that can stand alone, so acquiring syllable-level skills requires children to attend to the sounds in language separate from meaning—an important aspect of phonological knowledge. The ability to detect, segment, and count syllables is more important to reading acquisition than the ability to manipulate and transpose them (Adams, 1990).

Syllable Level Assessment

Assessment at the syllable level can be accomplished through a variety of tasks. The following assessment includes three types of syllable-level tasks: Blending, Tapping, and Deleting (see the Appendix for a blank assessment form). In the Blending Syllables task, pronounce a multisyllable word one syllable at a time and ask the student to say the whole word (e.g., "What word do these sounds make? *com . . . pu . . . ter*"). Pronounce words by segmenting syllables at natural auditory breaks rather than following dictionary rules for syllabication. For example, say "hopp-ing" or "hŏ-pping" but *not* "hop-ping." For the Tapping Syllables task, the student taps one time for each

A Sound Beginning

Phonological Awareness Assessment

SKILL: Blending Syllables

DIRECTIONS: For each item, say each word with a clearly discernible pause between syllables. **I'm going to say a word one part at a time. I want you to listen carefully, then put the parts together to make a whole word. Ready? Let's try one.**

PRACTICE ITEM: What word do these sounds make? 'can-dy' [candy]

TEST ITEMS:	ANSWER	(+/–)
1. tea-cher	teacher	+
2. hopp-ing	hopping	+
3. va-ca-tion	vacation	+
4. mo-tor-cy-cle	motorcycle	–
5. re-fri-ger-a-tor	refrigerator	+
	Blending Syllables Score	**4/5**

SKILL: Tapping Syllables

DIRECTIONS: Follow the procedures for tapping words in the previous section. Begin by modeling how to tap the syllables in the child's name. **We can tap the parts of your name.** [Model using child's name.] **Now you tap the parts in your name. Let's try another one.**

PRACTICE ITEM: COMPUTER [3 taps]

TEST ITEMS:	ANSWER	(+/–)
1. ALLIGATOR	4 taps	+
2. PAPER	2 taps	+
3. JUMP	1 tap	–
4. DINOSAUR	3 taps	+
5. BASKET	2 taps	+
	Tapping Syllables Score	**4/5**

SKILL: Deleting Syllables

PRACTICE ITEM: Say WONDER. Now say WONDER without saying DER.

TEST ITEMS:	ANSWER	(+/–)
1. Say SANDWICH. Now say SANDWICH without saying SAND.	(WICH)	+
2. Say PENCIL. Now say PENCIL without saying CIL.	(PEN)	+
3. Say ELBOW. Now say ELBOW without saying EL.	(BOW)	–
4. Say ANSWERING. Now say ANSWERING without saying ING.	(ANSWER)	+
5. Say REMEMBER. Now say REMEMBER without saying RE.	(MEMBER)	–
	Deleting Syllables Score	**3/5**
	Total Syllable Level Score	**11/15**

FIGURE 5.1 Sample syllable level phonological awareness assessments

syllable in the given word (e.g., medicine = three taps). In Deleting Syllables, the student pronounces a word and then says it again without a particular syllable (e.g., Say *pencil*. Now say *pencil* without saying *cil.*). Each of these tasks reveals a different type of phonological ability and helps determine the focus for instruction.

Syllable Level Activities

Even very young children can enjoy and benefit from activities at the syllable level. Teaching students to segment multisyllable words into individual syllables can begin in kindergarten or preschool. This process can be made into a game in which children separate their names or the names of their friends or familiar objects into syllables.

Instruction may begin with segmentation of compound words (e.g., football, outside, sidewalk). Children may also be taught to count the number of syllables in other long, but familiar words (e.g., refrigerator, motorcycle). These tasks require auditory attention and memory.

Even with young children, syllable-level activities may be incorporated into the school day and tied to instruction in other content areas. For example, when learning about community helpers, a kindergarten class might also clap out the name of each occupation (e.g., doc-tor; po-lice off-i-cer, lett-er carr-i-er). When teaching initial graphing skills in mathematics, a first-grade teacher might group children by the number of syllables in their first names and demonstrate how to graph this information. Word lists with two-syllable, three-syllable, and four-syllable words, as well as words with more than four syllables may be found in the Appendix.

TARGET SKILLS

❑ Blending Syllables
❑ Segmenting Syllables

ACTIVITIES

❑ Tapping Syllables
❑ Highlighting Syllables
❑ Counting Syllables with Picture Cards
❑ Junk Box Rock
❑ Hopscotch
❑ Syllable Sorting
❑ Toss It in the Toy Box!
❑ Puppet Play
❑ Go Fish!
❑ Guess My Word

Tapping Syllables

Target Skill

Segmenting syllables

Materials

Rhythm sticks

Sandpaper blocks

Other percussion instruments

Directions

Children tap out the syllables in words with rhythm sticks. This activity is implemented just as Tapping Words in the previous section. The teacher calls out a word, the child repeats the word and taps once for each syllable. Begin with longer words with multiple syllables; words with more syllables are easier than short words, particularly words with only one syllable.

Variation: Clap or tap out the number of syllables in a child's name. Begin with the first name, then clap first and middle names, and finally clap first, middle, and last names. This is a good activity for the beginning of the school year to help children learn their peers' names.

My name is Ziggy

Highlighting Syllables

Target Skill

Blending syllables

Segmenting syllables

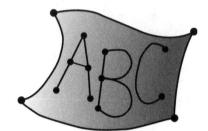

Materials

Books

Charts

Poems

Songs

Highlight tape

Overhead markers

Directions

After reading a book, poem, or song, go back through the story and find words with a specified number of syllables. Using highlight tape, cover the words in the chart or book. Go back to each highlighted word and clap or tap the syllables. After segmenting the syllables, blend the parts together to form the whole word.

Variation: Make this a whole-class activity by using a poem or song printed on large chart paper or an overhead transparency. Instead of using highlight tape, use assorted colored markers and circle the words chosen to highlight. For example, circle one-syllable words in blue, two-syllable words in red, and so on.

Counting Syllables
with Picture Cards

Target Skill

Segmenting syllables

Materials

Picture card file

Beanbag

Directions

ACTIVITY 1:

Give each student or group of students a set of cards. Have the students sort the cards into categories according to the number of syllables in each word.

ACTIVITY 2:

Select a picture card from the stack and ask the children to clap or tap the number of syllables in the word. This activity is perfect for circle time or fill time during transitions.

ACTIVITY 3:

Give each child a card. Have students sort themselves based on the number of syllables in the picture name. This activity can be used to group students for cooperative activities, or as a strategy to have students line up (e.g., "Line up for lunch quietly if your picture has three syllables").

ACTIVITY 4:

Playing beanbag toss is another variation of counting syllables. With children seated in a circle, begin the game by tossing the beanbag to the student seated on one side. The student then claps out the syllables in the teacher's name. The beanbag can also be tossed back and forth between two students as they segment a word into syllables (i.e., the beanbag is tossed for each syllable in the word).

Junk Box Rock

Target Skill

Segmenting syllables

Materials

Fill a box with common objects that have multisyllabic names.

Directions

Call on a child to pick an item from the box. The child names the item and does the "junk box rock" by rocking his/her hips from side to side for each syllable.

Variation: Instead of doing the junk box rock, have children march in place in the same manner. Use the names of various objects around the classroom or around the school. As you walk to different areas of the school grounds, march the syllables in the objects you see.

Variation: Junk Box Rock at the phoneme level. Instead of rocking for each syllable in the word, rock for each phoneme in the word.

5.5

Hopscotch

Target Skill

Segmenting syllables

Materials

Sidewalk chalk or hopscotch mat

Beanbag

Picture card file

Directions

Draw a hopscotch board with sidewalk chalk. Stack the picture cards face down in a pile at the beginning of the hopscotch board. Have the first player draw a card from the deck, say the name of the picture on the card, and segment the word into syllables. The player then tosses the beanbag to the corresponding square on the hopscotch board and hops the squares as in a traditional hopscotch game.

Variation: Play phoneme level hopscotch. Play in the same manner except that the words are segmented into phonemes instead of syllables. You will want to arrange your picture cards for the game variations. The syllable-level game should consist of picture cards with longer, multisyllable words, while the phoneme set should consist of words more easily segmented at the phoneme level.

Syllable Sorting

Target Skill

Segmenting syllables

Materials

Picture card file (Index cards with pictures from magazines or old workbooks. The cards should depict objects with multisyllabic names.)

Directions

Give each student or group of students a set of cards. Have the students sort the cards into categories according to the number of syllables in each word.

Variation 1: Have students clap out the number of syllables in the words illustrated on each card.

Variation 2: Give each child a card. Then have the students group themselves based on the number of syllables in the picture name.

Variation 3: Rather than using picture cards, use plastic toys and have students sort on a game board as shown in the picture below.

Toss It in the Toy Box!

Target Skill

Segmenting syllables

Materials

Toy boxes numbered

Plastic toys

Directions

Give each child a toy. Have them count the number of syllables in the toy. In turn, have them toss their toy into the appropriate toy box. For example, if a child has a frisbee, she would place it in the toy box labeled "two." Continue in turn until all children have tossed their toys into the toy boxes.

Variation: Create a toy box game board. Have five toy boxes on a poster board, each numbered. Use picture cards to sort the toys by syllable. If the toy on the picture card has one syllable, the card is placed above the #1 toy box. Picture cards can be self-correcting by writing the correct number on the back of each card.

Puppet Play

Target Skill

Syllable blending

Materials

Word list (Multisyllable words)

Puppet

Directions

Explain that your puppet says words one part at a time. You need some help determining what your puppet is saying. Have the puppet state words segmented into syllables, one syllable at a time. Ask the children to help the puppet by putting the parts together to say the whole word. For example, the puppet says, "com-pu-ter." Children respond, "computer."

Go Fish!

Target Skills

Segmenting syllables

Materials

Picture card file organized with four cards each of one to five syllables

Directions

This game is played like the traditional card game, Go Fish, and is designed for three to four players. Using your picture card file, create a deck of cards that have four cards each of the following: (1) one-syllable words, (2) two-syllable words, (3) three-syllable words, (4) four-syllable words, and (5) five-syllable words. The dealer deals five cards to each player. The remaining cards are placed face down to form a stack. The player to dealer's right begins. In turn, a player asks another specific player for their cards with a certain number of syllables. For example, the first child on his turn might say: "Willie, please give me your four-syllable words." The player who asks must already hold at least one card of that type, so Willie must hold at least one four-syllable word card to make this request. If the player who was asked (Willie) has cards of the named rank, he 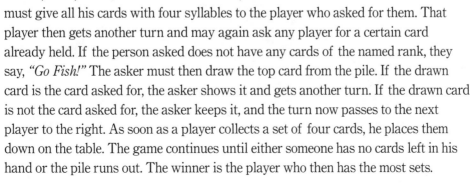 must give all his cards with four syllables to the player who asked for them. That player then gets another turn and may again ask any player for a certain card already held. If the person asked does not have any cards of the named rank, they say, *"Go Fish!"* The asker must then draw the top card from the pile. If the drawn card is the card asked for, the asker shows it and gets another turn. If the drawn card is not the card asked for, the asker keeps it, and the turn now passes to the next player to the right. As soon as a player collects a set of four cards, he places them down on the table. The game continues until either someone has no cards left in his hand or the pile runs out. The winner is the player who then has the most sets.

5.10

Guess My Word

Target Skills

Blending syllables

Materials

Syllable word lists (Appendix)

Directions

Using the syllable word list from the appendix, select a word and say the first syllable aloud. See if children can guess the word after you've said only the first syllable. Likely, the children will need another clue, so continue adding one syllable at a time giving the children an opportunity to guess the word after each syllable.

Encourage children to blend each word part as you say it aloud. For example, for the word *motorcycle,* say *mo* and give the children an opportunity to guess the word. Then say *tor* and give the children another opportunity to guess the word. If they cannot guess the word, model how to blend the first two syllables ("*mo* and *tor* makes *motor*") before saying *cy*. When you segment words into syllables, be sure to pronounce each syllable as it's pronounced in the word.

One of the purposes of this game is to encourage children to blend successive word parts as they go, rather than waiting until they have heard all of the parts to begin blending. To ensure that children develop this skill, you may need to provide extensive modeling.

CHAPTER SIX

The Onset-Rime Level

Adams (1990) discusses an intermediate and instructionally useful level of analysis between the syllable and the phoneme—the onset and rime level. The *onset* is the part of the syllable that precedes the vowel (e.g., the *c* in *cat,* the *br* in *brown*). The *rime* is the rest of the syllable (e.g., the *og* in *dog,* the *ack* in *black*). Because the rime is the part of the syllable that contains the vowel, all syllables must have a rime, but not all syllables have an onset (e.g., *and, out, or*).

Onset-rime segmentation skill is an essential component of phonological awareness development (Adams, 1990; Bryant, MacLean, Bradley, & Crossland, 1990). In spelling, children make more errors with consonants at the end of words or with consonant blends than with initial or medial consonants (Treiman, 1985). This finding suggests that children naturally segment words at neither the syllable nor the phoneme level. In addition, most children spell rimes more accurately than individual vowel sounds, which illustrates the level at which they are attending.

Treiman (1985, 1991, 1992) promotes the use of instruction at the onset and rime, or intrasyllabic, level. Because tasks that require onset and rime analysis require the segmentation of syllables, they are more sophisticated than syllable-level tasks. Yet these same tasks are easier than phoneme-level tasks because they do not require discrimination between all of the individual phonemes in a syllable. Onset-rime tasks could, therefore, be considered an intermediate step in the development of phonological awareness. The difficulty that many children experience when progressing from syllabic analysis to phonemic analysis may arise because the intermediate step, the intrasyllabic unit, is often omitted from early reading instruction. Providing experience working with onsets and rimes may alleviate this difficulty.

Onset-Rime Level Assessment

Although rhyming is typically one of the earliest phonological skills that children develop, children's levels of conscious understanding about rhyming vary. There are several types of skills related to phonological awareness at the onset-rime level, and thorough assessment includes measurement of multiple onset-rime skills. As with any assessment, teachers should begin with easier skills and move to more challenging tasks. Before beginning assessment, it is also helpful to determine whether the child understands the concept being measured. Some children can perform rhyming tasks but do not consciously understand what rhyming is.

Teachers sometimes make the mistake of explaining to children that rhyming words are words that sound the same at the end. A child who takes this explanation literally will believe that the words *hat* and *sit* rhyme, because they sound the same at the end. To make the concept clearer, explain that rhyming words sound the same in the middle and the end, but be sure to demonstrate. Without a demonstration, this explanation can be just as confusing for some children. For example, say "Do *cat* and *hat* rhyme? Yes, *cat* and *hat* rhyme. *Cat* has an /at/ and *hat* has an /at/. They both have an /at/, so they rhyme. Do *cat* and *sat* rhyme? . . . Do *lip* and *nip* rhyme? . . . " As with any initial instruction in a concept, it is helpful to use nonexamples to clarify what *is* a rhyme and what is *not* a rhyme. After providing multiple examples of rhyming words, ask children "Do *cat* and *cap* rhyme?" Because these words have several sounds in common, many children will mistake them for rhyming words. Just as in the previous example, follow the questions with a demonstration: "Let's see, *cat* has an /at/, does *cap* have an /at/? No, *cat* has an /at/, but *cap* has an /ap/, so *cat* and *cap* do not rhyme."

The following assessment measures three types of onset-rime level skills: rhyme matching, onset-rime blending, and rhyme generation (see the Appendix for a blank version of this assessment form). In the first task, rhyme matching, the child is simply asked to determine whether two words rhyme, just as in the previous example. In the second task, the teacher provides the sounds in a one-syllable word segmented into its onset and rime. The child blends the onset with the rime to pronounce the whole word.

Billy struggled to rhyme words throughout kindergarten. Now, in first grade, he was thoroughly frustrated whenever anyone asked him to rhyme words.

One day, Ms. Corbett asked Billy, "Can you tell me what rhyming words are?"

Billy had no idea how to answer. Ms Corbett sat down with him, pulled out some magnetic letters, and asked him to spell his name. When he had spelled B-i-l-l-y, Ms Corbett said, "Now, change the 'B' in 'Billy' to an 's.' What word do you have?"

"Silly," replied Billy.

Ms. Corbett continued, "That's right, it's 'silly.' Now, what part of the word stayed the same in 'Billy' and 'silly'?"

"I left 'illy' the same."

"What would happen if I changed the 's' in 'silly' to an 'h'? What word would you have?" Ms. Corbett asked.

After 'hilly,' 'chilly,' 'Willy,' and 'frilly' Ms. Corbett asked, "What is the same about all of these words?"

Billy replied, "They all have an 'illy' in them."

"That's right, and that's what makes them rhyming words. They all sound the same in the middle and at the end. They all have an 'illy' in them, so they rhyme."

Billy was puzzled. "Really? *That's* all there is to it?"

"That's all there is to it! What if we wanted to come up with words that rhyme with 'sat'? What part of the word would stay the same?"

Billy was ecstatic, "The 'at' would stay the same! Like in 'hat' and 'cat' and 'bat'!"

"That's exactly right! You have it now!"

Billy's problem was never that he was incapable of rhyming. He simply needed someone to take the time to make the concept of rhyming explicit for him.

A Sound Beginning

Phonological Awareness Assessment

ONSET/RIME LEVEL

SKILL: Matching Rhymes

PRACTICE ITEM: Do these two words rhyme: sack/black?
Do these two words rhyme: beat/bean?

TEST ITEMS:	ANSWER	(+/–)
1. Do these two words rhyme? hill/still	yes	+
2. Do these two words rhyme? drip/drop	no	+
3. Do these two words rhyme? jump/bump	yes	+
4. Do these two words rhyme? dock/rock	yes	+
5. Do these two words rhyme? day/cake	no	–
	Matching Rhymes Score	4/5

SKILL: Blending Onsets and Rimes

PRACTICE ITEM: What word do these sounds make? n-ote

TEST ITEMS:	ANSWER	(+/–)
1. f-an	fan	+
2. s-ip	sip	+
3. c-at	cat	+
4. st-op	stop	+
5. d-ance	dance	+
	Blending Onsets and Rimes Score	5/5

SKILL: Generating Rhymes

PRACTICE ITEM: Tell me a word that rhymes with *sat*. (Accept any rhyming word or pseudoword.)

TEST ITEMS:	(+/–)
1. Tell me a word that rhymes with *mop*.	+
2. Tell me a word that rhymes with *run*.	–
3. Tell me a word that rhymes with *name*.	+
4. Tell me a word that rhymes with *tip*.	+
5. Tell me a word that rhymes with *sell*.	–
Generating Rhymes Score	3/5
Total Syllable Level Score	12/15

FIGURE 6.1 Sample onset-rime level phonological awareness assessments

In the third task, the teacher provides a word and asks the child to provide a second word that rhymes with the first one (e.g., "Tell me a word that rhymes with *book*."). By mid-kindergarten, most children are able to perform these tasks successfully. Difficulty with any of these tasks may indicate a phonological awareness deficit in need of remediation.

Onset-Rime Level Activities

The most common onset and rime level activities are those involving rhyming or word families. Learning nursery rhymes and rhyming songs and poems helps develop this level of phonological awareness. This level is particularly useful for both assessment and initial instruction. Children who have difficulty at this level are very likely to struggle with phoneme level activities. The following pages contain suggested activities for developing phonological awareness at the onset-rime level. In addition, word lists with phonogram word families for onset-rime level activities is provided in the Appendix.

TARGET SKILLS

- ❏ Matching Rhymes
- ❏ Generating Rhymes
- ❏ Recognizing Rhyme
- ❏ Blending Onsets and Rimes

ACTIVITIES

- ❏ Word Bird
- ❏ CLUMP!
- ❏ Rhyme Around the Room
- ❏ Rhyme Time
- ❏ Word Family Blending Wheels
- ❏ Rhyming Pairs
- ❏ Croak
- ❏ Rhyme Detective
- ❏ Rhyme Pockets
- ❏ Alphabet Sponging
- ❏ Rhyme Around the Rosy
- ❏ Rhyming Memory
- ❏ Rhyming Bingo
- ❏ Building Words
- ❏ Shared Storybook Reading

Word Bird

Target Skills

Generating rhymes

Materials

Bird beanbag or Hacky sack

Directions

Have children stand in a circle and you stand in the middle of the circle. Toss the "bird" to a child and call out a word. The child tosses the "bird" back and calls out a word that rhymes with the teacher's word. For example, toss the beanbag to the first student and say, *"BOAT."* The child tosses the beanbag back and says, *"GOAT."* Continue by going around the circle and providing each child the opportunity to generate a rhyming word. (Hint: It is helpful to have a list of words ready, or cards from the picture card file rather than trying to come up with words for rhyme quickly.)

Variation 1: Challenge the students to see how quickly they can work around the circle. Start a timer and then begin the rhyming game. When the "bird" has made it all the way around the circle, then stop the timer. The students can try to beat their time the next time around the circle.

Variation 2: Instead of the child throwing the beanbag back to the teacher, the child hands the beanbag to the next child, who comes up with another rhyming word. The class tries to get all the way around the circle generating rhymes (words or nonwords) with the initial target word. For example, begin tossing the word bird and say, "BOAT," the first child says, "GOAT," the next child says, "VOTE," the next one "MOAT," the next one "GLOAT," the next one "SOAT." Remind the children that the words can be real words or silly words.

Variation 3: Using picture cards, place the cards (one per student) face down in the middle of the circle. Have one child begin by standing in the center of the circle and drawing a card from the top of the pile. This picture card is the target word. The child then calls out the target word and tosses the beanbag to a classmate. The child responds with a rhyming word and the two children trade places. The second child draws the next card from the pile and the game continues until all the children have had a turn generating a rhyme.

CLUMP!

Target Skill

Matching rhymes

Materials

Picture card file

Directions

Give each child a card from the picture card file. After everyone has the opportunity to look at their card say, *"CLUMP!"* The children quietly walk around the room and get into a small clump with children who have a word that rhymes with their picture card. Children can CLUMP to creatively group cooperative learning groups.

Variation 1: Give each child three picture cards, each on a different color card (e.g., a red card, a blue card, and a yellow card). Then say, *"CLUMP BLUE!"* Children look at the blue card and clump with their friends with rhyming words on the blue cards. Next say, *"CLUMP RED!"* Again, children clump by finding peers with rhyming red picture cards. Repeat until children have clumped with all three cards.

Variation 2: Clump by syllables. For example, call out a category such as first name. Children will clump by the number of syllables in their first names. Other syllable clumping categories include first and last names, a parent's first name, or home street.

Rhyme around the Room

Target Skill

Generating Rhymes

Materials

Fill a box with small toys

Directions

Pick up an item from the room. Call on a child and ask him to say a word that rhymes with the object you selected. Continue to go around the room and ask children to provide rhyming words.

Variation 1: This variation is similar to Junk Box Rock described in the Syllable Level activities section. Fill a box with small toys and objects. Call on a child to pick an item from the box. The child names the item and calls out a word that rhymes with the object.

Variation 2: Play the game I SPY! with rhyming words. You say, "I spy something that rhymes with *blue*." Ask the students to guess what you spy. "You spy the *glue*!"

Rhyme Time

Target Skills

Recognizing rhyme

Generating rhyme

Materials

None

Directions

ACTIVITY 1: Rhyme recognition

Children can be taught to determine if two one-syllable words rhyme. Some children have an inherent knowledge of rhymes based on extensive experiences with language and print. Other children who have not developed this knowledge may need explicit instruction about what a rhyme is (i.e., words rhyme when they sound the same in the middle and at the end). It is also helpful to think aloud about rhyming. Consider the following example: Do *cat* and *hat* rhyme? Let's think. *Cat* has *at,* does *hat* have *at*? Yes, *cat* and *hat* both have *at,* so they rhyme. This instruction should be accompanied by numerous examples and non-examples of rhymes. Rhyme recognition simply requires the student to recognize a pair of rhyming words presented orally.

ACTIVITY 2: Rhyme generation

Generating a word or list of words that rhyme with a given word is more difficult than determining if two given words rhyme. The additional cognitive and language requirements of rhyme generation make it quite challenging for some children. The ability to generate rhymes, however, is an excellent indicator of a child's ability to apply phonological knowledge. Many children engage in sponta-neous word games that use rhyming skills. This fun way to practice skills should be encouraged.

Word Family Blending Wheel

Target Skills

Blending onsets and rimes

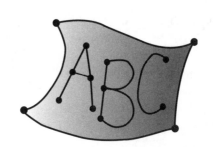

Materials

Brass fasteners

Word family wheel pattern (see Appendix)

Card stock

Directions

Construct a word family wheel by copying the pattern from the Appendix onto thick card stock. Cut the window from the front pattern. Place the wheel behind the pattern so that the onset peeks through the window. Attach the wheel with the brass fastener. Turn the wheel to reveal various onsets. The rime remains constant on the front of the pattern. The child blends the onset and rime together to form various words and pseudowords.

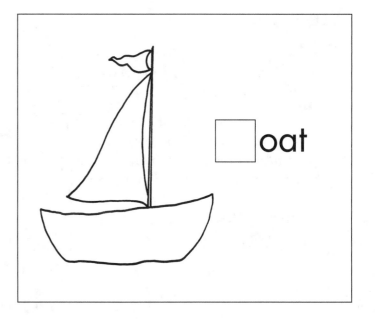

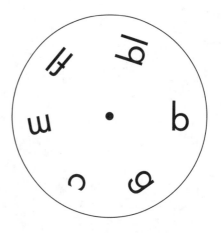

Rhyming Pairs

Target Skills

Recognizing rhyme

Generating rhyme

Blending onsets and rimes

Materials

Chart of poem with rhyming stanzas

Alphabet stamps and ink pad

Directions

Cover the second rhyming word in each couplet or stanza. Post the poem and read aloud with students. Stop at each covered word and solicit a response from a student in the class.

Variation: Using the inkpad and stamps, have a student stamp the word in the covered blank using the alphabet stamps. This is more appropriate for a small-group activity.

To market, to market
to buy a fat pig.
Home again, home again
jiggity- ⬚ .
To market, to market
to buy a fat hog.
Home again, home again
jiggity- ⬚ .

CROAK!

Target Skills

Generating rhyme

Materials

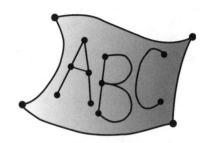

Croak cards (see Appendix)

Opaque container (cup or can)

Timer (optional)

Directions

Make CROAK cards using small strips of cardstock paper. The cards should have a variety of words for which the children can generate a rhyme (e.g., day, go, map, hat, bug). For every six to ten word cards, make one card with the word CROAK on it. Place the cards in the container.

In turn, each child draws a card from the container. If the card has a word on it, the child reads the word and thinks of a rhyming word. If he is able to generate a rhyming word, he keeps the card. If the card has CROAK on it, he returns all his cards to the can. This game can be played in a specified amount of time by setting a timer. When the timer goes off, the child with the most cards wins. An alternative would be to end the game when one child has a set number of cards (e.g., first one with five cards wins).

Variation: For younger students, use cards that depict various objects instead of word cards. Play the game in the same manner as described above.

Rhyme Detective

Target Skills

Matching rhyme

Materials

Picture card file

Directions

ACTIVITY 1: Oddity Detection

This task requires children to indicate which in a list of three or four words does not rhyme with the other words in the list. The familiar song from the television show *Sesame Street* does this well: "Which of these words is not like the others? Which of these words just doesn't belong?"

ACTIVITY 2: Rhyme Matching

Given a list of three or four words, students indicate which one from the list rhymes with a target word. For example, given stamp, map, lip, and lamp, a student would match stamp and lamp.

ACTIVITY 3: Rhyme Matching with Pictures

For these activities, children are asked to look at pictures and generate the sounds themselves by naming the word the picture represents. Students match pictures illustrating words that share a common rhyme. This activity is somewhat more advanced than activities that begin with the teacher generating the sounds, because some students find it more difficult to detect individual phonemes when they do not hear the word.

Rhyme Pockets

Target Skills

Recognizing rhyme

Materials

Hanging pocket chart

Picture cards in rhyming pairs

Directions

Place one set of picture cards in pockets, and provide a student with a set of matching rhyme cards. The student matches each card in his stack with the rhyming word in the pocket chart and places his card in the appropriate pocket. This makes an excellent center activity and can be made self-checking by putting corresponding symbols on the back of the cards with rhyming pairs.

Alphabet Sponging

Target Skills

Generating rhyme

Blending onsets and rimes

Segmenting onsets and rimes

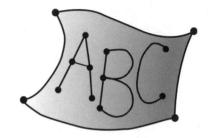

Materials

Alphabet shaped sponges

Construction paper

Water

Plastic storage bags

Directions

Select a word family and gather the appropriate onset and rime sponges needed to make words. For example, if you are working on the word family "at," use the following sponges: a, t, s, b, c, f, h, m, p, and r. Moisten the sponges and place them in plastic storage bags. Students use the moistened sponges to create words on the construction paper. Store different word family sets in different bags. When the first word family dries, students can trade bags and create a new set of words.

Rhyme around the Rosy

Target Skills

Generating rhyme

Materials

Chairs organized in a circle

Deck of picture cards

Directions

Organize the students' chairs in a circle and place the deck of picture cards face down under one chair. Students stand in front of their chairs and sing the song Ring Around the Rosy changing the words "Ring" to "Rhyme" and "fall" to "sit." The song would go like this: *"Rhyme around the rosy, pocket full of posies, ashes, ashes, we all sit down."* Children sit at the appropriate point in the song. The student who sits in the chair with the picture card deck takes the first card from the pile, names the picture, and gives a word that rhymes with the picture. Repeat the game allowing each child to end up in the picture card seat.

Rhyming Memory

Target Skills

Recognizing rhyme

Materials

Picture cards with rhyming pairs (twenty pairs)

Directions

Shuffle the cards and place them face down in a matrix layout (e.g., four rows of five cards). Children take turns selecting two cards. If the pair rhymes, they keep the pair. Play continues until no more cards remain on the board.

Variation: Play memory at various levels of phonological awareness. Organize your picture cards with word pairs for number of phonemes or number of syllables. A matching pair would be any two cards with the same number of the target (i.e., either phoneme or syllable).

Rhyming Bingo

Target Skills

Recognizing rhyme

Materials

Bingo cards

Markers

Directions

Make Bingo cards with pictures of objects representing common word families (e.g., *boat, cat, pig, frog*), leaving one word out for calling card and placing rhyming words on various Bingo cards. As you call out a word, students check their cards for a matching rhyme. Continue, following the traditional Bingo format.

Variation: Make Bingo cards with words on cards instead of pictures. Call out a word and have students find the rhyming word.

6.14

Onset-Rime
Building Words

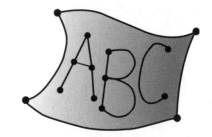

Target Skill

Blending onsets and rimes

Segmenting onsets and rimes

Materials

Small alphabet cards for each student or magnetic letters

Card holder (optional)

Onset-rime level building words chart (see Appendix)

Directions

Choose a list from the Building Words Chart in the Appendix. At the top of each word list, the required letters are specified. Give each student a set of alphabet cards and a cardholder. List the letter cards that the children will need on the chalkboard or overhead transparency. Students display the required letters on the desk in front of their cardholder. The teacher then calls out the word and has the student "build" the word on the cardholder. The teacher then asks the children to change the word by manipulating the onset. For example, if the students have built *mat*, the teacher could say, "Now, change *mat* and make *map*." The children would then change the *t* to a *p* and build the new word. Continue in this manner until each word on the list has been built.

Shared Storybooks

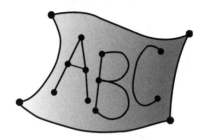

Target Skills

Generating rhyme

Detecting rhyme

Materials

Storybooks with multiple rhyme patterns (see list in the Appendix)

Directions

Rhyming activities can be effectively embedded in read-aloud time. Select books with multiple rhyme patterns. Several strategies can be included to help children grasp the concept of rhyme. For example, as you read books with rhyme patterns, enunciate rhyming pairs. After reading a rhyming pair, point out the rhyme, "Listen, honey and money rhyme!" A third strategy is to allow the children to predict the second word in a rhyming pair. Read the first line and enunciate the first word in the rhyming pair; then pause and let the children respond to finish the second line with the word that rhymes.

CHAPTER SEVEN

The Phoneme Level

Phonemes are the smallest units of spoken language, usually represented in print by single letters or by digraphs. The English language consists of between forty and forty-eight phonemes. This range reflects the variety of dialects in the pronunciation of sounds in English. Although some individual phonemes form words (e.g., a, oh, eye), most words are composed of a series of phonemes (e.g., c-a-t, i-tch-y, s-p-l-a-sh).

Phonemes are generally classified into two major categories: consonants and vowels. There are approximately twenty-five consonant sounds in English. Most consonant sounds are represented by a single letter, such as *b, t,* or *m.* Some consonant sounds are spelled with two letters, such as *ch, sh,* or *th.* Some consonant letters have more than one common pronunciation (e.g., *c, g*). Still other consonant letters, such as *x* and *q* (or more properly, *qu*), represent a combination of sounds (x = /ks/; *qu* = /kw/). Consonant phonemes are produced by restricting airflow from the mouth. If airflow is only partially restricted, as in *s, m,* or *v,* the phonemes are called a *continuous* sound. Continuous sounds can be elongated without distortion. If the airflow is stopped completely, as in *t, b,* or *k,* the phoneme is considered a *stop* sound. Stop sounds cannot be elongated without distortion. During the pronunciation of some consonants (e.g., *b, d, m, v*), the vocal cords vibrate; these are called *voiced* sounds. During the pronunciation of other consonants (e.g., *s, k, p*), the vocal cords are still; these are called *unvoiced* sounds.

There are approximately eighteen vowel sounds in English, and five letters (*a, e, i, o, u*) represent most of these sounds. All vowel sounds are *voiced,* and they are characterized by unrestricted airflow from the mouth. Vowels differ from one another by the position of the tongue in the mouth (i.e., high or low, front or back, middle) and by the shape of the mouth itself (i.e., rounded or stretched lips, tense or loose facial muscles). The sounds of vowels are most commonly classified as "long" or "short" or, sometimes, "r-controlled" vowels. In addition, vowel sounds can be represented by two letters together, called *digraphs* (e.g., *ai, ea*). *Diphthongs* are two letters combined to make a single, gliding vowel sound, such as *ou* or *oi.*

Because the differences among vowel sounds are more subtle than the differences among consonant sounds, some children experience much more difficulty working with vowels. Understanding the distinctions between pronunciations of sounds can aid children in the development of sensitivity to or awareness of individual phonemes in words. Conscious sensitivity to the individual phonemes in words is necessary for skilled decoding.

Phonemic Awareness

As discussed in Chapter 1, the term *phonemic awareness* is frequently—but incorrectly—used interchangeably with *phonological awareness,* a much broader construct. While phonological awareness includes awareness of words, syllables, onsets and rimes, and phonemes, phonemic awareness applies only to phoneme-level awareness. More specifically, phonemic awareness is the ability to attend to and manipulate sounds at the phoneme level. Phonemic awareness skills include the ability to detect, segment, and blend phonemes and to manipulate their position in words (Adams, 1990; Armbruster, Lehr, & Osborne, 2001; Lenchner et al., 1990).

Phonemes are impossible to segment in a pure sense. During speech, phonemes are formed and blended in such a way that one phoneme's production is influenced by the surrounding phonemes. For example, say the words *cat* and *cot,* and pay attention to the shape of your mouth as you pronounce the /k/ sound. The /k/ sound is formed differently in these two words due to the influence of the vowel that follows it. We perceive the same sound at the beginning of the two words, although there are measurable differences. Difficulty understanding when slight differences such as these are significant enough to be considered a different sound is one factor that makes phoneme-level skills difficult for some children. Because phonemic analysis requires the reader to detect, segment, and manipulate individual phonemes, it is a much more sophisticated task and, consequently, a much more difficult task than either syllabic or intrasyllabic analysis (Treiman, 1991, 1992).

Research on phonemic awareness. Most of the research on phonological awareness instruction has focused on the phoneme level. Numerous intervention studies designed to increase phonemic awareness have resulted in gains in reading and spelling (e.g., Ball & Blachman, 1991; Bradley & Bryant, 1983; Byrne & Fielding-Barnsley, 1995; Cunningham, 1990; Iversen & Tunmer, 1993; Lundberg et al., 1988).

The National Reading Panel (2000), in its report on teaching children to read, identified phonemic awareness as a critical aspect of early literacy development. The panel conducted a meta-analysis of phonemic awareness studies and came to several important conclusions. They determined that there is clear and compelling evidence that phonemic awareness can be taught effectively under a variety of conditions and with a variety of learners. They also concluded that phonemic awareness instruction helps children become better readers at both word reading and comprehension levels. The panel found that phonemic awareness instruction also helps children become better spellers, although the effects for children with reading disabilities is weaker than for other children. Finally, as previously mentioned, the panel determined that teaching phonemic awareness with letters is more effective than instruction without letters. These conclusions can be used to inform early literacy instruction.

Phoneme-level skills. Phoneme-level skills include sound detection, matching, deletion, blending, segmenting, and manipulation. Skills in blending and segmenting phonemes are the most sophisticated associated with phonological awareness and the most important for application to decoding (Adams, 1990). Blending and segmenting may be taught in a variety of ways. One of the most useful methods for helping young children to understand the concepts of phonemic blending and segmentation is teaching them to "converse" with a puppet or toy robot in a "secret language." Torgesen and Bryant (1994) used this approach in *Phonological Awareness Training for Reading,* but the method is easy to adapt to informal instruction. The idea is that the puppet or robot can only say words or can only understand words when they are said one sound at a time. Young children seem to accept and understand this explanation quite readily and are eager to try communicating in this unusual fashion. A complete sequence of lessons using this technique is included at the end of this chapter.

When teaching or assessing blending and segmentation skills, the teacher should be careful to completely segment phonemes before blending them. Many teachers have the tendency simply to say a word slowly, drawing out the phonemes. When children learn to decode, it is necessary for them to identify the sounds of separate letters and then to blend those letter sounds together. Previous oral blending practice is helpful for students when they are ready to become more fluent with decoding skills.

Phoneme pronunciation. Children with reading disabilities also make significantly more speech production errors, and these errors can be attributed to deficits in phonological processing (Catts, 1986). Children who lack sensitivity to the sound structure of language make phonological errors during speech as well as during reading. Inaccurate practice during speech may facilitate the formation of inappropriate sound associations, causing both speech and reading problems.

Teachers should be careful to pronounce individual phonemes in a manner that will make them "blendable." Many teachers, in an effort to make short or "stop" consonant sounds more audible, add a vowel sound to the consonant. This additional sound, usually a schwa or short *u* sound, distorts the consonant sound, making it very difficult to blend with other phonemes. For example, a *b* may be incorrectly pronounced "buh," and a *t* may be incorrectly pronounced "tuh." Blending the letters *b, a,* and *t* then produces "buh-a-tuh," and most children have serious difficulty identifying the word. It is important to pronounce these stop consonants as quickly as possible, without the confusing "uh." Because it is impossible to pronounce a voiced stop consonant such as *b* or *d* in isolation with no vowel sound attached, the teacher should model saying the sound with an extremely brief short *i* sound following it. The place in the vocal anatomy where the short *i* is produced is closer to the location of more of the other sounds than the short *u*. Teaching children to use this strategy helps them blend stop consonants more readily.

Calling Attention to How a Sound Is Produced

Ms. Barnes turns to her group and says, "Say the sound for 'm' with me. Ready? /mmm/. Good. What was your mouth doing when you said the /mmm/ sound?"

Hannah responds, "My lips were together."

"That's right! Your lips were together. If your lips were together, though, how did the air come out?"

Derek ponders, "Through my nose?"

"Well, let's see about that! Everyone, say the /mmm/ sound. Now, keep saying /mmm/, but hold your nose. What happened to the sound?"

"It stopped!" the children reply.

"That's right! The sound stopped, because the air comes through your nose. When you held your nose, you stopped the air and that stopped the sound. That's because the /mmm/ sound comes through your nose."

Another way to alleviate this problem is to begin instruction in blending and segmenting using only words with continuous consonant sounds (e.g., s, v, z, f, m, n, sh, th) at the beginning position. These sounds are much easier to blend than the stop consonants, and their use in early instruction makes the skill of blending more accessible for children. As children are introduced to blending skills, stop consonants may be used at the end of words. In the final position, stop consonants are easier to pronounce quickly and with little distortion. When students become competent with pronunciation of stop consonants at the end of a word, the introduction of stops at the initial position becomes less troublesome.

Phoneme Level Assessment

A multitude of assessment instruments designed to measure phonemic awareness is available. The following assessments demonstrate a fairly simple method for measuring phoneme blending and segmenting skills. In the first assessment, the teacher pronounces words sound by sound, and the child blends the sounds together to form a real word. In the second assessment, the teacher pronounces a complete word, and the child segments the word into its component sounds. It is especially helpful to conduct these two assessments in sequence. That is, the blending assessment should be conducted first, and the segmenting assessment should be conducted immediately after. The segmenting task is difficult for many children, but much of the difficulty lies in some children's lack of understanding regarding the task. By conducting the two assessments in sequence, the teacher can use the blending task as an example of what to do in the segmenting task (e.g., "Now I want you to say the words sound by sound, like I did in the last word game we played.").

Phoneme Level Activities

Most instruction designed to develop phonological awareness quite appropriately focuses on the phoneme level. The phoneme level of phonological awareness is the most critical to reading and spelling. When reading or decoding a word, a child must say each sound in the word and blend the sounds together. When spelling or encoding a word, the child must segment the sounds in the word and then represent each sound with a letter.

In the following activities, phoneme blending and segmenting are the primary focus, but other skills such as deleting, inserting, and matching phonemes are developed, as well. Some of the activities make clear connections to print, either by using letters during blending and segmenting practice or by practicing skills in connected text. Phonemic awareness activities that include letter-sound work can be considered phonics instruction.

TARGET SKILLS

- [ ] Blending Phonemes
- [ ] Segmenting Phonemes
- [ ] Deleting Phonemes
- [ ] Matching Phonemes
- [ ] Inserting Phonemes
- [ ] Manipulating Phonemes
- [ ] Detecting Phonemes

ACTIVITIES

- [ ] Sound Detective
- [ ] Oddity Detection
- [ ] Sound Play
- [ ] Elkonin Boxes
- [ ] Sound Around
- [ ] Bead Counting
- [ ] Sorting Game
- [ ] Sound Splash
- [ ] Sound Bingo
- [ ] I Spy!
- [ ] Sound Flips
- [ ] Sound Clues
- [ ] Phoneme Level Building Words
- [ ] Round We Go
- [ ] Sound Hound
- [ ] Sound Off!
- [ ] Sound Train
- [ ] Frog Hop
- [ ] Sound Bites
- [ ] Robbie the Robot

A Sound Beginning

Phonological Awareness Assessment

PHONEME LEVEL

SKILL: Blending Phonemes

DIRECTIONS: Stop administering when child misses 5 items in a row. Segment sounds as indicated by a (-) in each item. Be sure to pause briefly but discernibly between segmented sounds. If the child asks you to repeat the sounds, you may do so.

If the child says the sounds separately (e.g., m-e, rather than me) prompt by saying, **Try to say the sounds altogether as a real word.** This prompt may be used as often as needed on practice items only.

PRACTICE ITEMS: I'm going to say a word in small parts. I will say one part of the word at a time. I want you to listen carefully, then put the parts together to make a whole word. Ready? Let's try one. What word do these sounds make? 'l-i-p'

If correct: **That's right. Let's try the next one.**
If incorrect: **That's not quite right. When you put 'l-i-p' together, it makes 'lip.' Let's try the next one.**

Continue to give corrective feedback as above. **What word do these sounds make: i-t? What word do these sounds make: m-a-t?**

Let's try some more words. Each time, I will say a word one part at a time. Listen carefully and put the parts together to make a whole word.

TEST ITEMS: (provide no more feedback)

		(+/−)
1. n-o	no	+
2. i-f	if	+
3. sh-e	she	+
4. s-u-n	sun	+
5. c-a-p	cap	+
6. b-o-th	both	−
7. f-a-s-t	fast	+
8. j-u-m-p	jump	−
9. s-t-ar-t	start	−
10. s-p-l-a-sh	splash	−
	Blending Phonemes Score	6/10

FIGURE 7.1a

Sample phoneme level phonological awareness assessments

A Sound Beginning

Phonological Awareness Assessment

SKILL: Segmenting Phonemes

DIRECTIONS: Stop administering when child misses 5 items in a row. **I am going to say a word. I want you to break the word apart and say it sound by sound, like I did in the last word game we played. For example, if I say DAY, you would say it sound by sound, D-AY. Now you say the word DAY sound by sound.**

If correct: **That's right. You have the idea. Let's try the next one.**

If incorrect: **That's not quite right. To say DAY sound by sound, say D-AY. Let's try the next one.**

PRACTICE ITEMS: (continue corrective feedback) **Remember, I will say a word, then you say it sound by sound.**

a. no	n-o
b. it	i-t
c. pie	p-ie

Let's try a few more. I will say a word, then you say it sound by sound.

TEST ITEMS: (no feedback)   (+/–)

1. go	g-o	+
2. up	u-p	+
3. me	m-e	+

DIRECTIONS: Now we are going to do some words that have more sounds in them. Let's try a few for practice. (Give corrective feedback as on previous practice items.)

PRACTICE ITEMS:

a. mat	m-a-t
b. good	g-oo-d
c. winner	w-i-nn-er

TEST ITEMS: (no feedback)   (+/–)

4. back	b-a-k	+
5. mop	m-o-p	–
6. pig	p-i-g	+
7. stop	s-t-o-p	–
8. smoke	s-m-o-ke	–
9. toast	t-oa-s-t	–
10. mother	m-o-th-er	–

Segmenting Phonemes Score 5/10

Total Phoneme Level Score 11/20

FIGURE 7.1b

Sound Detective

Target Skills

Detecting phonemes

Matching phonemes

Materials

Words

Picture cards

Directions

ACTIVITY 1: Sound detection

Given a target phoneme, students determine which words on a list begin or end with that sound (e.g., "Give a 'thumbs up' for each word that begins with a /d/: *dog, find, dish, Dan, . . .* ").

Variation: This activity can be used during story or passage reading, as well. While reading connected text, students find all words in the selection that include the target phoneme. As students become comfortable with beginning and ending sounds, activities that include detection of a target medial sound should be added.

ACTIVITY 2: Sound matching

To match sounds, students must determine which in a selection of words begins or ends with the same sound as a given word. For example, you may ask students, "Which word begins with the same sound as *cat: corn, must,* or *wish*?" As students master this skill, the activity should be modified to request ending or middle sound matching, and more words may be added to the list.

ACTIVITY 3: Sound matching using pictures

Ask children to look at picture cards and generate the sounds themselves by naming the word the picture represents. Students match pictures illustrating words that share a common initial, medial, or final phoneme. This activity is somewhat more advanced than activities that begin with the teacher generating the sounds, as some students find it more difficult to detect individual phonemes when they do not hear someone else say the word.

Oddity Detection

Target Skills

Detecting phonemes

Matching phonemes

Materials

Picture cards

Directions

In this activity, the student is expected to generate the name of the word the picture represents. The student then determines which picture in a set of pictures illustrating words does not share a common initial, medial, or final phoneme. These activities should begin targeting the initial phoneme, followed by the final phoneme. Work with medial sounds should begin when students become skilled with beginning and ending sounds.

ACTIVITY 1: Oddity detection using pictures

Organize picture cards into sets of three so that each set has two similar and one odd picture based on a single characteristic (e.g., words with common initial, medial, or final phonemes). Show students one set at a time, and ask them to determine which card does not belong.

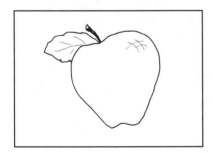  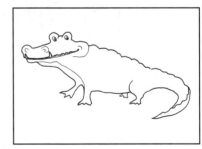

ACTIVITY 2: Oddity detection with sounds

The procedures for this activity are very similar to those for oddity detection using pictures. The difference, however, is that students are asked to determine which in a list of words begins or ends with a sound different from a given word. For example, you may ask, "Which of these words does not have the same ending sound as cat: mutt, lift, cake, or bite?"

Sound Play

Target Skills

Deleting phonemes

Inserting phonemes

Directions

Phoneme deletion and insertion activities require students to detect and manipulate sounds in a word. Students are asked to supply an initial consonant when it is deleted from a word or to delete a specified sound from a target word. For example, you may say, "Say mat. Now say mat without saying the /t/ sound." Table 7.1 provides examples for *Sound Play*.

TABLE 7.1 Examples for Sound Play

INSTRUCTION	EXAMPLE
Deleting Phonemes	
Say *meet*. Now say *meet*, but don't say /t/.	me
Say *for*. Now say *for* but don't say /f/.	or
Say *tree*. Now say *tree* but don't say /r/.	tee
Say *spot*. Now say *spot* but don't say /s/.	pot
Inserting Phonemes	
Say *an*. Now say *an* with a /f/ at the beginning.	fan
Say *Ben*. Now say *Ben* with a /t/ at the end.	bent
Say *mile*. Now say *mile*, but add an /s/ to the beginning.	smile
Say *high*. Now say *high* with a /k/ at the end.	hike

7.4

Elkonin Boxes

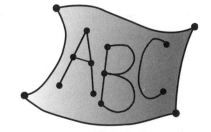

Target Skills

Segmenting phonemes

Blending phonemes

Materials

Picture cards

Counters

Directions

ACTIVITY 1: Counting phonemes

Elkonin (1963) introduced a method of developing phonemic segmentation skills that has become quite popular in recent years. This method involves the use of Elkonin boxes—picture cards with boxes under each picture representing the number of phonemes in that word (see Appendix for samples). While saying the word slowly, sound-by-sound, the student moves a counter into each box to represent each sound in the word. This activity may be modified to allow the teacher and student to practice the skill orally. Demonstrate using fingers to count phonemes, raising one finger as each phoneme is pronounced. With teacher guidance, the student should be able to learn how to count phonemes independently.

ACTIVITY 2: Counting phonemes and writing letters

Help the student count the sounds in a word and draw the appropriate number of boxes on the practice page. Select only words that have few sounds and that have regular spellings. Begin by having the student put counters into the boxes as described above. Then ask him to identify the letter that makes the first sound and prompt him to write that letter in the first box. Help the student identify the letter that corresponds to each sound and write it in the appropriate box. If the student needs a model of how to write the letter, show him a magnetic letter or a letter card with the letter. At first, do not emphasize the order of the sounds. Let the student enter the letters he knows, and provide the other letters for him. For example, a child may be able to detect the first and final sounds in the word, but not the medial sound. You would then provide the medial sound. As he becomes more confident with this procedure, begin to require that he enter the letters in the correct order from beginning to end.

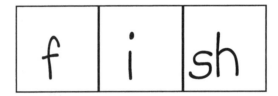

Variation 1: As you move from words with regular, simple spellings to words with more difficult spellings, you may need to put more than one letter in a box to represent a single sound. Use this opportunity to point out to the student that several letters often work together to make one sound and some letters are silent.

Variation 2: To help the student progress to spelling more difficult words independently, use dotted lines to split those boxes in which two letters are required to make one sound.

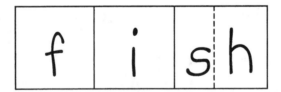

After sufficient practice with each of these activities, the student should be able to make his own boxes when needed. Eventually, the student should be able to spell the words using the sounding-out techniques without the Elkonin boxes.

Sound Around

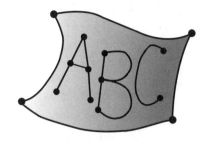

Target Skills

Blending phonemes

Segmenting phonemes

Manipulating phonemes

Materials

Large word cards

Phoneme level building words chart (see Appendix)

Directions

Create large letter cards for a set of words using the building words chart. As the teacher calls out a word from the list, the students who have the corresponding letter cards stand side-by-side to make the word. Students move around to match the sounds in the words the teacher calls.

Variation: Once students become comfortable with manipulation of sounds represented with one letter, provide cards with digraphs. Provide every child in the class with a card, and challenge them to find classmates with whom they can form words. Encourage them to make nonsense words as well as real words.

Variation: Instead of using letter cards, have children manipulate phonemes in words using the sounds only. For example, begin by having three children stand in the front of the room. Introduce each child, "Class, this is /t/. Who is this?" [Children respond, "/t/"] "Good. Now meet /i/. Who is this?" [Children respond]. "And this is /p/. Who is this?" [Children respond.] "If I put /i/ and /t/ together [place children side-by-side], what word would I have?" Children respond, "IT!" "What if I put /p/ before /it/? Then what would I have?" Children respond, "pit." Then have /t/ and /p/ trade places and ask the children to figure out the new word.

Bead Counting

Target Skills

Segmenting phonemes

Blending phonemes

Materials

Beads

Cord

Word cards

Directions

Make individual bead strings with six beads on approximately ten inches of cord (older students will enjoy making their own bead counters). String the beads on the cord and tie a knot at each end. Call out a word card from the deck of word cards. Have students use their bead counters to count the number of phonemes in the word. Then you count the phonemes and the students check their bead strings.

Variation: Students can use marker boards and dry erase markers to draw Elkonin boxes after they have used the bead strings to count the phonemes. They can then represent each phoneme with the appropriate letter. Magnetic letters also work well; instead of writing the graphemes in the Elkonin boxes, use the magnetic letters.

7.7

Sorting Game

Target Skills

Detecting phonemes

Matching phonemes

Materials

Sorting game board

Picture cards or small plastic toys

Number cards

Directions

Using the sorting game board, have children sort the toys or picture cards based on the following targets:

ACTIVITY 1: Matching sounds sorting

Select pictures or toys to be sorted based on matching beginning sounds. Select three to five toys or pictures with various beginning sounds (e.g., ball, tiger, fish). Place each item on the game board. Ask the child to select a toy or picture card and sort by matching the beginning sound.

ACTIVITY 2: Counting sounds

Place the number cards on the game board. This game can be played one-on-one or in small groups. Have the first child select a toy or picture card, segment the word into phonemes, and place the card or toy on the corresponding number card. Take turns allowing each child to select a card and segment phonemes. Children can segment the word individually or together as a group.

Sound Splash

Target Skills

Segmenting phonemes

Materials

Picture card file

Twister game *or* Splash Mat

Spinner

Picture cards

Directions

Create a Splash Mat using a blue plastic tarp or shower curtain liner. Draw or paint lily pads in a pattern similar to the Twister game and write numerals on each lily pad, or simply modify the traditional Twister game by writing numerals on the circles on the mat. The object of the game is to stay on the lily pads and not "splash" into the pond. Place the "Splash Mat" on the floor. The caller spins the spinner and draws a card from the deck. The spinner indicates either left or right, and hand or foot. The caller calls out the name of the word on the card and a hand or foot. If you're playing at the syllable level, the child puts the appropriate hand or foot on a lily pad with the numeral matching the number of syllables in the word called out. Play is continued until only one person remains standing.

7.9

Sound Bingo

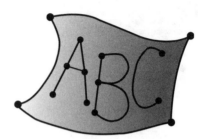

Target Skills

Detecting phonemes

Materials

Sound Bingo cards (see Appendix)

Markers

Letter/sound cards (see Appendix)

Directions

Provide each child with a sound bingo card and several markers. Shuffle the letter/sound cards. Draw one letter/sound card and ask children to find a picture of something that begins with that sound. For example, if you draw the *sh* card, you would say, *"Can you find a picture of something that begins with /sh/?"* The children would then place the marker on a picture of a shoe, or a ship, etc. Play continues until one child covers the entire board.

To make sound bingo cards, select pictures that represent the following list or similar objects. Place the pictures on the grid randomly.

TABLE 7.2   **Sound Beginning Bingo**

SOUND CARD	PICTURES			
sh	shoe	ship	shell	shark
t	tiger	tooth	television	two
s	sun	sign	star	six
f	fan	finger	five man	flag
r	rabbit	rhinoceros	rose	ring
m	monkey	moon	moose	man

I Spy!

Target Skills

Detecting phonemes

Materials

No specific materials required

Directions

Find an item in the classroom that begins with a target sound. Say *"I spy something that begins with /t/."* Children try to guess the object you "spy." A variation of this game is to play using students' names. During circle time, say "I spy someone whose name begins with /t/." Again, have children guess which of their classmates you spy. After children are confident in detecting the initial phoneme in words, play the game and have children detect the final phoneme, *"I spy something that ends with /t/,"* or *"I spy something that ends like cat."*

7.11 Sound Flips

Target Skills

Blending phonemes

Materials

Three-ring binder

Cardstock or poster board

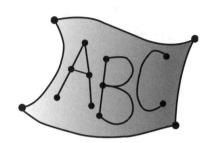

Directions

Create sound flips by using a three-ring binder and card stock. Using a three-hole punch, punch a stack of card stock paper, and cut the stack into thirds (each strip should be $8^{1}/_{2}'' \times 3^{2}/_{3}''$). Place each set of strips into the three-ring binder. Write beginning sounds (consonants or consonant blends) on the first set of cards. On the second set, write medial sounds (vowels or vowel digraphs), and on the third set write final sounds (see table below). Have children flip the cards and

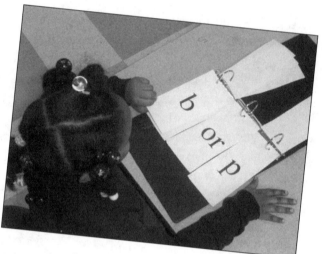

blend the sounds together. The sound flips will form real and nonsense words. Table 7.3 provides examples of graphemes for the sound flip cards.

TABLE 7.3 Letters for Sound Flips

CARD SET ONE BEGINNING SOUNDS	CARD SET TWO MEDIAL SOUNDS	CARD SET THREE FINAL SOUNDS
b	a	b
c	e	st
f	i	d
d	ea	t
st	oa	sh
t	o	p

Sound Clues

Target Skills

Blending phonemes

Materials

Sound clue riddles

Directions

Create riddles for your class to solve using sound clues. Read the riddle aloud, stating the answer sound by sound. Ask the children to blend the sounds together to solve the riddle. Several sound clues are provided in Table 7.4. Use these sound clues or create your own.

TABLE 7.4 **Examples of Sound Clues**

RIDDLE	ANSWER
You can see me at night, when I shine bright. I am the /m/ /oo/ /n/.	moon
I come out in the day so that you can play. I am the /s/ /u/ /n/.	sun
Flip a switch and I shine bright. I am a /l/ /igh/ /t/.	light
I come in twos. I am /sh/ /oo/ /z/.	shoes
Put me in the water and I will float. Now you know that I am a /b/ /o/ /t/.	boat

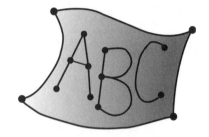

7.13 Building Words

Target Skill

Blending phonemes

Segmenting phonemes

Materials

Small alphabet cards for each student or magnetic letters

Card holder (optional)

Phoneme Level Building Words Chart (see Appendix)

Directions

Choose a list from the *Phoneme Level Building Words Chart* in the Appendix. At the top of each word list, the required letters are specified. Give each student a set of alphabet cards and a cardholder. List the letter cards that the children will need on the chalkboard or overhead transparency. Students display the required letters on the desk in front of their cardholder. Call out the word and have the student "build" the word on the cardholder. Then ask the children to change the word by manipulating the onset. For example, if the students have built *mat,* you could say, "Now, change *mat* and make *map*." The children would then change the *t* to a *p* and build the new word. Continue in this manner until each word on the list has been built.

7.14

Round We Go

Target Skills

Detecting phonemes

Materials

Grab bag of various objects (e.g., small plastic animals)

Directions

Arrange chairs in a circle, or have children sit on the floor in a circle. Select an object from the grab bag and hand it to one child, and then turn on music. The children pass the item around the circle until the music stops. When the music stops the child with the toy gives a word that begins with the same beginning sound as the toy that is being passed around the circle. A new object is drawn and the music starts again. Children can sing, *"Round and round and round we go, where it stops nobody knows,"* as they pass the toy around the circle.

Sound Hound

Target Skills

Matching phonemes

Materials

Sound Hound card

Picture card file

Directions

This game, created after the popular game Old Maid, is designed for play with a small group of children (three to four). Deal all cards between players. Cards are made from the picture card file and consist of twenty pairs (matches of beginning sounds) and one Sound Hound card. Play begins to the right of the dealer. If the player has any matches (pairs of cards with the same beginning sound), he places the pairs on the pair board. He then takes a card from an opponent. If he has a card with the same beginning sound, he places the pair on the board. Play continues until all pairs have been matched and one player ends up with "Sound Hound." "Sound Hound" is the dealer for the next game.

Sound Off!

Target Skills

Segmenting phonemes

Materials

40 picture cards (cards should represent words of various lengths and with various numbers of phonemes)

Directions

This game is designed for two players and is played like the popular card game, War. One player deals the cards evenly between the two players (twenty cards each). Each player turns over a card and counts the phonemes in the word pictured. The player that has the most phonemes in his word takes the pair. If the players have a picture with the same number of phonemes, they have a *SOUND OFF*. Each player places two cards face down, and a third face up. The players compare phonemes and the player with the word with the most phonemes takes all the cards. The game ends when one player ends up with all of the cards.

Sound Train

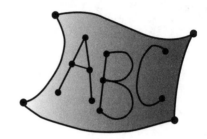

Target Skills

Detecting sound

Matching sound

Materials

Sound train engines and boxcars (see Appendix)

Directions

Make sound trains using the patterns found in the Appendix. Copy the boxcars multiple times. Cut out pictures and glue them to the boxcars. Place the engines on the wall or magnetic board. Give each child a boxcar with a picture on it. The children determine which engine matches their boxcar. For example, if the boxcar has a picture of a ship, it would go on the /sh/ engine. In turn, each child places her boxcar on the appropriate engine.

Variation 1: Use the sound train to help children line up for lunch or recess. For example, say, "If your boxcar begins with the /sh/ sound, place it on the engine and line up for lunch." Continue until all children have built their trains and are in line for lunch.

Variation 2: Glue pictures to the engine cards, and create letter cards with the boxcars. Give each child a letter card and have students build the trains. For example, an engine card might have a bus pictured on it. The child with the 'b' boxcar would first place his card on the engine, then the child with the 'u', and so forth until the words are built on the sound trains.

7.18

Frog Hop

Target Skills

Segmenting phonemes

Materials

Frog Hop game board

Picture card file

Directions

Create a *Frog Hop* game board using green circle stickers and construction paper or a file folder. Create a standard game board with a start and a finish. Use the green circle stickers as lily pads. Decorate the game board to look like a pond. In turn, each student draws a card from the picture card pile, counts the number of phonemes and moves his game piece that many lily pads. So after drawing a card with a cat pictured, the child would jump three lily pads for /k/ /a/ /t/. The first one to the finish line wins.

START

Frog Hop

Sound Bites

Target Skills

Deleting phonemes

Materials

Puppet

Directions

Select puppets and give them alliterative names (e.g., Sammy Shark, Leo Lion, Tom Turtle). The puppets will take sound bites out of words based on their names. For example, Sammy Shark loves to bite the /s/ out of words. Select words from Sammy's word list below. Say to the children, "I had a word. The word was *slip*. But Sammy bit the /s/ off slip, so what do I have left?" The children should respond with "lip." Continue with the other words from Sammy's word list. Generate similar lists to match the puppets you have.

Sammy's word list: slip, star, slime, smile, street, fast, must, faster, desk, list

Robbie the Robot

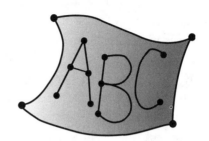

Target Skills

Segmenting phonemes

Blending phonemes

Materials

Robbie the Robot (see Appendix)

Lesson scripts (see Appendix)

Stories (see Appendix)

Target sound list (see Appendix)

Directions

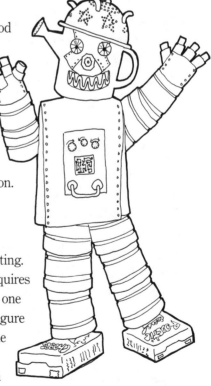

The Robbie the Robot lessons provide a simple, fun method of teaching students the most important phonological skills: blending and segmenting. Sample lessons (Appendix, page 139) are scripted to demonstrate the direct instruction method of teaching the skills. This method is used to ensure that the presentation of skills is clear and explicit and that each student has an opportunity to master each skill. Torgesen and Bryant (1994) introduced the use of a picture of a robot as a vehicle for initial instruction. Kids love this approach, and they don't even know that their skills are improving.

This sequence of lessons uses a picture of a robot as a stimulus for explaining the concepts of blending and segmenting. The premise is that communicating with Robbie the Robot requires the student to blend and segment. Robbie can only say words one sound at a time, which requires students to blend sounds to figure out what he said. He can also only understand words when the student says them one sound at a time, which requires the child to segment sounds. For young children, this explanation of blending and segmenting tends to be very accessible.

The first three lessons in the sequence are used to introduce blending and segmentation skills to students. In lessons 4 through 13, students practice these skills using target consonants to learn to apply these skills in context. Lessons 14 through 18 introduce vowels and rhyming skills.

The purpose of these lessons is twofold. Students should (1) acquire the basic phonological skills needed for skilled reading, and (2) learn how these phonological skills are applied during decoding. Teachers should not assume that all readers will generalize the isolated skills instruction to the application level. Students with very poor reading fluency have particular difficulty acquiring and applying these skills. Explicit instruction in how to apply skills is important to promote this type of generalization. This intervention was designed for use with first-grade students, but the lessons may be adapted for older or younger students.

Instructional groups of three to six students are recommended. The instructor should ensure that each student in the group has sufficient practice to master skills during each lesson. Additional practice with peers may promote skills mastery, as well. Each lesson should last approximately fifteen to twenty-five minutes, depending on group size and skill level.

Throughout each lesson script, the instructor's directions for what to *say* are in bold type. Directions for what to *do* are in parentheses. The expected student responses are in italics. Pacing of lessons should be quick, but should allow sufficient time for each student to practice and master the skills. Instruction may vary from the script, but each component of the script should be included.

The Appendix includes the passages and target sound word lists. Each passage was written specifically to emphasize a particular target sound. These passages have been used successfully with first-, second-, and third-grade students. It is perfectly acceptable to use other passages to practice the application of phonological skills. Beginning with the original passages and moving on to other children's literature may provide students with the necessary controlled practice that will promote skill acquisition.

Promoting Generalization

After completing the 18 lessons, help students apply these skills to other passages. At first, choose passages that have a frequently occurring target sound. Practice blending, segmenting, and rhyming the words in isolation, and guide the students in reading the passage. Practice this procedure often, with a variety of progressively longer passages. This allows students to learn how to apply their phonological skills to decoding in context. Emphasize how these phonological skills can be applied to students' independent decoding during reading. After students have developed this skill, prompt them to apply it during reading whenever they come to an unfamiliar word.

Variation: Robbie the Robot can be used at anytime during the day to allow students to practice blending and segmenting. Once children begin interacting with Robbie, he'll be added fun for your class all day!

CHAPTER EIGHT

Phonemic Awareness and Phonics

Phonemes (sounds) are represented by graphemes (letters). In some cases, a single phoneme might be represented by a variety of graphemes (e.g., the "long e" sound may be spelled as *e, ea, ee, ie, i, ei,* or *ey*), and in other cases a single grapheme might represent a variety of phonemes (e.g., the letter *s* may be pronounced as /s/, /z/, /sh/, or /zh/). Instruction that promotes understanding of the relationship between phonemes and graphemes is called phonics instruction.

The distinction between phonemic awareness and phonics is confusing for many educators. Although phonemic awareness and phonics are both critical aspects of literacy development, they are different constructs. Phonemic awareness is the understanding that words can be broken into individual sounds. Phonics instruction teaches the connections between letters and sounds. Phonics instruction requires exposure to print or, more specifically, to letters. Phonemic awareness instruction can be conducted with or without letters, and many activities that develop phonemic awareness involve no letters. When letters are included, it becomes phonics instruction. Phonics instruction can help a child increase phonemic awareness, but without some level of phonological awareness, that child is unlikely to benefit from phonics.

For many years, reading teachers would identify children in their classrooms who just could not "do" phonics. Despite their best efforts, teachers could not get these children to understand the alphabetic principle—the insight that letters and sounds work together in systematic ways to form words. Because they knew it was educationally sound practice to teach to students' strengths, these teachers, upon recognition that a child could not "do" phonics, would teach the child to read words by sight. This form of instruction by sight words, whether drill and practice with flash cards or repeated reading of connected text, would produce children who had large sight word vocabularies but no strategies to identify unknown words, unless the context made the identity of the word clear. This resulted in children who had inefficient processes for accessing unfamiliar text. Research in the 1980s and 1990s demonstrated clearly that children who cannot "do" phonics are almost invariably weak in phonological awareness. This research also demonstrated that weaknesses in phonological awareness can be corrected, and these improvements usually translate to improvements in reading ability. Now, when a teacher identifies a child who can't "do" phonics, a more likely route to intervention is to address the child's fundamental weakness: phonological awareness. This approach, which is becoming more and more common in schools, is a much more effective means to improved reading outcomes for children.

Research has demonstrated that phonemic awareness instruction that includes work with letters is more effective than instruction without letters (Hatcher et al., 1994; Iversen & Tunmer, 1993; National Reading Panel, 2000; Torgesen, Wagner, & Rashotte, 1997). In other words, phonics instruction is one of the best ways to improve phonemic awareness. To accomplish this, however, phonics instruction must emphasize for children more than just letter-sound correspondences. Practice blending, segmenting, and manipulating sounds through letter play can be a very powerful way to develop sensitivity to the sound structure of words.

An examination of what occurs as a child decodes a word makes the connection between phonological awareness and phonics more clear. Stahl (2002) explains that decoding a regular word involves recognizing letters, attaching a sound to each letter, and blending the sounds to form a word. The first two steps in this sequence, identifying letters and connecting sounds to those letters, represent aspects of the alphabetic principle. The final step, blending sounds to form a word, is a phonological skill that can be performed even in the absence of print. Likewise, spelling involves three steps: segmenting a word into individual sounds, attaching a letter to each sound, and forming the letters on the page. The first step, segmenting the word into sounds, requires phonological awareness. For many children, difficulties with decoding or spelling words can be attributed to weak phonological awareness.

> "Despite evidence that one can develop phonological awareness outside the context of literacy instruction, there is considerable evidence that this instruction is enhanced when the connections to print are made explicit."
>
> —Blachman (2000, p. 487)

Manipulating Letters

Several techniques for phonics instruction include the manipulation of letters to teach blending and segmenting skills. The function of manipulative letters in reading instruction is thought to be similar to the function of manipulative objects in mathematics instruction. In math, manipulative objects are used to make abstract concepts more concrete and understandable (Mercer & Miller, 1992). In reading, the physical process of moving letters together and apart helps children understand the abstract concepts of phoneme blending and segmenting.

Patricia Cunningham has described a technique she calls "making words" (Cunningham, 1999). In this approach, children begin with a set of letter cards that spell a "mystery" word. The teacher guides children in the construction of a variety of smaller words, using the letters from the mystery word. Through this activity, children begin to understand how to add, delete, and substitute phonemes in words. Because they pair sounds with letters, they also develop their understanding of the alphabetic principle.

Tutorial models such as Reading Recovery (Clay, 1993) and the University of Florida Literacy Initiative (UFLI; Hayes, Lane, & Pullen, 1999) include manipulation of magnetic letters. In a study of instructional components of the UFLI model, word work with manipulative letters was shown to be the most critical factor in the development of children's decoding skills (Lane, Pullen, & Hudson, 2003). In this word work, children were taught to manipulate words at both the onset-rime and phoneme levels. They were also taught to encode (spell) words and decode (read) words with the manipulative letters. Finally, they did this work with both real words and nonsense words, to ensure that they were not relying on sight word knowledge to form words. Working with manipulative letters is a simple and effective method of teaching children to apply their phonological skills.

Sound Boxes

The process of using sound boxes (e.g., Elkonin boxes) to segment sounds was described in Chapter 7. As moving counters into the boxes shifts to writing letters, the process becomes phonics instruction. This method has been shown to be a very powerful method for helping children learn to segment phonemes in words (Clay, 1993; Joseph, 2000; Lane, Pullen, & Hudson, 2003). Particular techniques for using sound boxes can enhance their effectiveness (Hayes, Lane, & Pullen, 1999). For example, having children count the sounds in a word several times before writing the boxes focuses attention on the segmentation process. Drawing each box one at a time while saying the sounds once more emphasizes the connection between the counting activity and the individual boxes. Saying all the sounds in the word over and over as the child determines which sound goes where reinforces the segmentation process. Finally, writing the letter(s) for each sound enhances the student's understanding of the alphabetic principle.

The Relationship between Phonological Awareness and Phonics

One recurring question of early research on phonological awareness was that of causality. Does phonological awareness cause decoding abilities to develop? Or does decoding instruction (phonics) develop phonological awareness? Several studies demonstrated that the relationship is reciprocal (McGuiness, McGuiness, & Donohue, 1995; Perfetti, Beck, Bell, & Hughes, 1987). That is, phonological awareness instruction improves decoding skill and decoding instruction improves phonological awareness. Ultimately, however, a child must have some degree of conscious sensitivity to the sound structure of language before phonics instruction begins to make sense. A solid foundation of phonological skills makes phonics instruction much more accessible for children.

Phonological awareness instruction should never be considered an end in itself. It should always be conducted with its connections to decoding in mind. Likewise, phonics instruction can be easier for the teacher if appropriate efforts have been made to ensure that students have developed phonological awareness. Phonological awareness instruction "is about developing in children the attentional and metacognitive control that renders unnecessary" phonics drills (Adams, 2001, p. 76).

> " . . . although an awareness of the phonemic segments in spoken words will make it easier for a child to understand how an alphabetic orthography transcribes speech, this awareness does not come naturally for many beginning readers. "
>
> —Blachman (2000, p. 484)

The Relationship between Phonological Awareness and Phonics   **97**

CHAPTER NINE

Phonological Awareness as Part of a Comprehensive Reading Curriculum

Phonological awareness, although sometimes considered a precursor to reading, actually seems to be "intricately involved in early reading acquisition" (Stahl, 2002, p. 342). Phonological awareness is a critical component of reading instruction, but it does not constitute an entire reading program. The National Reading Panel (2000) cautions teachers to remember that acquiring phonological awareness is a means to an end, not an end in itself. Phonological awareness must be included in any comprehensive early reading curriculum, but it should only consume a few minutes per day of reading instruction.

Students' instructional needs will, of course, differ, and one child may need much more instruction than the next. Frequent and systematic assessment to monitor the progress of developing students can identify which children have continuing needs. These assessments may then be used to tailor instruction to meet individual learning needs.

> "Teaching children to manipulate phonemes in words is highly effective under a variety of teaching conditions with a variety of learners across a range of grade and age levels."
>
> —National Reading Panel (2000)

To ensure adequate progress with struggling students, phonological awareness skills should be taught *explicitly.* The instructional program must show children what they are expected to do. Teachers must model skills they want children to perform before the children are asked to demonstrate the skill. Such instruction may be designed as stand-alone activities or as part of other reading lessons.

Many of the activities described here can be integrated into any reading activity or used as games during instruction or during non-instructional time (Chard & Dickson, 1999). For example, singing and playtime activities offer many opportunities for kindergarten teachers to incorporate phonological skill development. Stories or poems that include rhyming words may be used as a tool to introduce and develop concepts and skills in rhyming. A teacher of older students could ask them to count the number of syllables or phonemes in the names of story characters or in new vocabulary words. If a teacher encourages the use of invented spellings, students learn to segment words and represent the correct number of phonemes. Modeling how to sound out a word to invent a spelling can help students develop these skills. As students learn about decoding, numerous other opportunities for instruction in blending and segmentation arise.

The teacher could make a simple whole-class game out of rhyme or phoneme matching (e.g., "Line up for lunch if your name rhymes with _____," or "if your name has a /t/ at the end."). Teachers can challenge students to think of words that have a particular number of syllables or phonemes. Finding many fun and innovative ways to include such sound play in the school day will address the instructional needs of some students. Additional explicit instruction and practice in specific skills will certainly be required for some students who have difficulty acquiring phonological skills, but such informal opportunities to practice throughout the day will help these students, as well.

Combining informal sound play and formal phonological awareness instruction during typical reading and writing activities for all students with explicit skill instruction for students who need additional practice should address the diverse needs in most elementary classrooms. The most important thing for teachers to do is to make the sound structure of language conspicuous to students who do not develop phonological awareness independently.

The activities presented in this book are designed to develop phonological awareness. Applying these auditory skills to reading requires students to have a working knowledge of sound-symbol relationships, which is typically acquired through phonics instruction. Phonics instruction can enhance phonological awareness, but some fundamental degree of phonological awareness is necessary for children to benefit from phonics instruction.

Reading research has clearly demonstrated the significance of phonological awareness in the development of early reading skills, and a variety of effective methods for assessment and instruction of phonological skills have been developed. Teachers in remedial and special education programs now have another tool for addressing students' reading problems. *All* teachers of young children must recognize the importance of incorporating phonological awareness into programs designed to promote emergent literacy, because these teachers now have a tool for *preventing* reading problems.

APPENDIX

Table of Appendices

A Sound Beginning

Phonological Awareness Assessment

STUDENT RECORD

Name: _____ Grade: _____

Date of Birth: _____ School: _____

Examiner: _____ Title: _____

Word Level

Date:

Tapping Words	/5	/5	/5
Deleting Words	/5	/5	/5
Total Word Level	/10	/10	/10

Syllable Level

Blending Syllables	/5	/5	/5
Tapping Syllables	/5	/5	/5
Deleting Syllables	/5	/5	/5
Total Syllable Level	/15	/15	/15

Onset-Rime Level

Matching Rhymes	/5	/5	/5
Blending Onsets and Rimes	/5	/5	/5
Generating Rhymes	/5	/5	/5
Total Onset-Rime Level	/15	/15	/15

Phoneme Level

Blending Phonemes	/10	/10	/10
Segmenting Phonemes	/10	/10	/10
Total Phoneme Level	/20	/20	/20

Total Score	/60	/60	/60

Observations

Date:	Date:	Date:

A Sound Beginning

Phonological Awareness Assessment

SKILL: Tapping Words

DIRECTIONS: Say words in bold to student. **In this word game, I want you to tap one time for every word you hear in my sentence. So, if I say, "*An apple is red,*" you tap like this."** [Model saying the sentence and tapping 4 times.] **Now you try.** Repeat with practice item and provide corrective feedback as needed. Do not provide corrective feedback on the test items.

PRACTICE ITEM: "The little frog is jumping."

TEST ITEMS:	ANSWER	(+/–)
1. Sue is my friend.	4 TAPS	_____
2. My mother is calling me.	5 TAPS	_____
3. The dog is chasing the kittens.	6 TAPS	_____
4. The boy is running.	4 TAPS	_____
5. She is wearing a purple jacket.	6 TAPS	_____
	Word Tapping Score	/5

SKILL: Deleting Words

PRACTICE ITEM: Say COWBOY. Now say COWBOY without saying BOY.

TEST ITEMS:	ANSWER	(+/–)
1. Say SAILBOAT. Now say SAILBOAT without saying SAIL.	BOAT	_____
2. Say APPLESAUCE. Now say APPLESAUCE without saying SAUCE.	APPLE	_____
3. Say SIDEWALK. Now say SIDEWALK without saying SIDE.	WALK	_____
4. Say SUNSHINE. Now say SUNSHINE without saying SUN.	SHINE	_____
5. Say CUPCAKE. Now say CUPCAKE without saying CAKE.	CUP	_____
	Word Deletion Score	/5
	Total Word Level Score	/10

A Sound Beginning

Phonological Awareness Assessment

SYLLABLE LEVEL

SKILL: Blending Syllables

DIRECTIONS: For each item, say each word with a clearly discernible pause between syllables. **I'm going to say a word one part at a time. I want you to listen carefully, then put the parts together to make a whole word. Ready? Let's try one.**

PRACTICE ITEM: What word do these sounds make? 'can-dy' [candy]

TEST ITEMS:	ANSWER	(+/−)
1. tea-cher	teacher	_____
2. hopp-ing	hopping	_____
3. va-ca-tion	vacation	_____
4. mo-tor-cy-cle	motorcycle	_____
5. re-fri-ger-a-tor	refrigerator	_____
	Blending Syllables Score	/5

SKILL: Tapping Syllables

DIRECTIONS: Follow the procedures for tapping words in the previous section. Begin by modeling how to tap the syllables in the child's name. **We can tap the parts of your name.** [Model using child's name.] **Now you tap the parts in your name. Let's try another one.**

PRACTICE ITEM: COMPUTER [3 taps]

TEST ITEMS:	ANSWER	(+/−)
1. ALLIGATOR	4 taps	_____
2. PAPER	2 taps	_____
3. JUMP	1 tap	_____
4. DINOSAUR	3 taps	_____
5. BASKET	2 taps	_____
	Tapping Syllables Score	/5

SKILL: Deleting Syllables

PRACTICE ITEM: Say WONDER. Now say WONDER without saying DER.

TEST ITEMS:	ANSWER	(+/−)
1. Say SANDWICH. Now say SANDWICH without saying SAND.	(WICH)	_____
2. Say PENCIL. Now say PENCIL without saying CIL.	(PEN)	_____
3. Say ELBOW. Now say ELBOW without saying EL.	(BOW)	_____
4. Say ANSWERING. Now say ANSWERING without saying ING.	(ANSWER)	_____
5. Say REMEMBER. Now say REMEMBER without saying RE.	(MEMBER)	_____
	Deleting Syllables Score	/5
	Total Syllable Level Score	/15

A Sound Beginning

Phonological Awareness Assessment

ONSET/RIME LEVEL

SKILL: Matching Rhymes

PRACTICE ITEMS: Do these two words rhyme: sack/black?
Do these two words rhyme: beat/bean?

TEST ITEMS:	ANSWER	(+/–)
1. Do these two words rhyme? hill/still	yes	_____
2. Do these two words rhyme? drip/drop	no	_____
3. Do these two words rhyme? jump/bump	yes	_____
4. Do these two words rhyme? dock/rock	yes	_____
5. Do these two words rhyme? day/cake	no	_____
	Matching Rhymes Score	/5

SKILL: Blending Onsets and Rimes

PRACTICE ITEM: What word do these sounds make? n-ote

TEST ITEMS:	ANSWER	(+/–)
1. f-an	fan	_____
2. s-ip	sip	_____
3. c-at	cat	_____
4. st-op	stop	_____
5. d-ance	dance	_____
	Blending Onsets and Rimes Score	/5

SKILL: Generating Rhymes

PRACTICE ITEM: Tell me a word that rhymes with *sat*. (Accept any rhyming word or pseudoword.)

TEST ITEMS:	(+/–)
1. Tell me a word that rhymes with *mop*.	_____
2. Tell me a word that rhymes with *run*.	_____
3. Tell me a word that rhymes with *name*.	_____
4. Tell me a word that rhymes with *tip*.	_____
5. Tell me a word that rhymes with *sell*.	_____
Generating Rhymes Score	/5
Total Syllable Level Score	/15

A Sound Beginning

Phonological Awareness Assessment

PHONEME LEVEL

SKILL: Blending Phonemes

DIRECTIONS: Stop administering when child misses 5 items in a row. Segment sounds as indicated by a (-) in each item. Be sure to pause briefly but discernibly between segmented sounds. If the child asks you to repeat the sounds, you may do so.

If the child says the sounds separately (e.g., m-e, rather than me) prompt by saying, **Try to say the sounds altogether as a real word.** This prompt may be used as often as needed on practice items only.

PRACTICE ITEMS: **I'm going to say a word in small parts. I will say one part of the word at a time. I want you to listen carefully, then put the parts together to make a whole word. Ready? Let's try one. What word do these sounds make? 'l-i-p'**

If correct: **That's right. Let's try the next one.**
If incorrect: **That's not quite right. When you put 'l-i-p' together, it makes 'lip.' Let's try the next one.**

Continue to give corrective feedback as above. **What word do these sounds make: i-t? What word do these sounds make: m-a-t?**

Let's try some more words. Each time, I will say a word one part at a time. Listen carefully and put the parts together to make a whole word.

TEST ITEMS: (provide no more feedback)   (+/–)

1. n-o	no	_____
2. i-f	if	_____
3. sh-e	she	_____
4. s-u-n	sun	_____
5. c-a-p	cap	_____
6. b-o-th	both	_____
7. f-a-s-t	fast	_____
8. j-u-m-p	jump	_____
9. s-t-ar-t	start	_____
10. s-p-l-a-sh	splash	_____

Blending Phonemes Score   */10*

A Sound Beginning

Phonological Awareness Assessment

PHONEME LEVEL

SKILL: Segmenting Phonemes

DIRECTIONS: Stop administering when child misses 5 items in a row. **I am going to say a word. I want you to break the word apart and say it sound by sound, like I did in the last word game we played. For example, if I say DAY, you would say it sound by sound, D-AY. Now you say the word DAY sound by sound.**

If correct: **That's right. You have the idea. Let's try the next one.**

If incorrect: **That's not quite right. To say DAY sound by sound, say D-AY. Let's try the next one.**

PRACTICE ITEMS: (continue corrective feedback) **Remember, I will say a word, then you say it sound by sound.**

a. no	n-o
b. it	i-t
c. pie	p-ie

Let's try a few more. I will say a word, then you say it sound by sound.

TEST ITEMS: (no feedback)   (+/–)

1. go	g-o	_____
2. up	u-p	_____
3. me	m-e	_____

DIRECTIONS: Now we are going to do some words that have more sounds in them. Let's try a few for practice. (Give corrective feedback as on previous practice items.)

PRACTICE ITEMS:

a. mat	m-a-t
b. good	g-oo-d
c. winner	w-i-nn-er

TEST ITEMS: (no feedback)   (+/–)

4. back	b-a-k	_____
5. mop	m-o-p	_____
6. pig	p-i-g	_____
7. stop	s-t-o-p	_____
8. smoke	s-m-o-ke	_____
9. toast	t-oa-s-t	_____
10. mother	m-o-th-er	_____

Segmenting Phonemes Score   /10

Total Phoneme Level Score   /20

A Sound Beginning

Phonological Awareness Assessment

Student Name	Date:					Date:					Date:				
	Word Level	Syllable Level	Onset-Rime Level	Phoneme Level	Total Score	Word Level	Syllable Level	Onset-Rime Level	Phoneme Level	Total Score	Word Level	Syllable Level	Onset-Rime Level	Phoneme Level	Total Score

A Sound Beginning

Invented Spelling Assessment

DIRECTIONS: Administer the following list as a "pretend" spelling. Let student know that the purpose of this test is to see how well he can sound out words. The examiner may begin by saying, "I know you haven't learned to spell these words yet, but I want you to sound them out and try the best you can." Encourage the student to attempt every word and to write as much as he knows about each word. To administer the test, say each word then read the sentence and, finally, repeat the word. Allow the student sufficient time to sound out each word carefully. Speed is not a factor in this test, and it is not necessary to administer all items in one sitting. Do NOT sound out words *for* the student. Spellings will be scored for phonological accuracy. If students already know the conventional spelling of a word, substitute another word with similar phonological features, and make a notation on the test.

1.	pretend	We can pretend we are old.	pretend
2.	float	The canoe will float down the river.	float
3.	while	Whistle while you work.	while
4.	ruler	We used a ruler to measure the paper.	ruler
5.	finish	Derek helped me finish my work.	finish
6.	angry	Mother was angry when we were late.	angry
7.	picking	The children were picking flowers.	picking
8.	junk	I cleaned the junk out of my closet.	junk
9.	planted	We planted a tree in the yard.	planted
10.	dress	Annie wore a blue dress.	dress

DIRECTIONS FOR SCORING: This assessment is scored based on phonological accuracy of each spelling. Points are awarded based on the scale below.

0 points	no phonemes accurately represented
½ point	1 phoneme other than the initial phoneme accurately represented
1 point	initial phoneme accurately represented
2 points	initial phoneme and one other phoneme accurately represented
3 points	initial phoneme and two or more phonemes accurately represented
4 points	phonologically accurate spelling

Connecting Words

Color in a box for each word your teacher reads in the sentence.

<table>
<tr><td></td><td></td><td></td><td></td><td></td><td></td><td></td><td></td></tr>
</table>

Croak Cards

day	pet	cap
sit	egg	dog
pig	zap	hat
spin	fan	sock
mug	map	song
lip	car	cow
see	meet	hop

Onset-Rime Building Words Chart

-at words a, b, c, e, f, h, m, p, r, s, t	-an words a, b, c, f, m, n, p, r, s, t, v	-ap words a, c, g, l, m, n, p, r, s, t	-ack words a, b, c, k, l, m, n, p, r, s, t
at	ban	cap	back
bat	can	gap	pack
cat	fan	lap	rack
fat	man	map	sack
hat	pan	nap	tack
mat	ran	rap	black
pat	tan	sap	crack
rat	van	tap	snack
sat	plan	clap	track
vat	scan	flap	shack
flat		slap	smack
that		snap	
		trap	

-ag words a, b, d, f, g, l, n, r, s, t, w	-ell words b, d, e, f, l, l, m, s, t	-et words a, b, e, f, g, j, l, m, n, p, s, t, v, w, y	-in words c, f, g, k, n, p, r, s, t, w
bag	bell	bet	fin
lag	fell	get	kin
nag	sell	jet	pin
rag	well	met	win
tag	shell	pet	chin
wag	tell	wet	grin
drag	smell	let	spin
flag	spell	set	skin
snag	dell	vet	thin
		yet	twin
		fret	

-ing words b, c, g, h, i, k, l, n, r, s, t, w	-op words b, c, d, h, m, o, p, p, r, s, t,	-ock words b, c, d, f, h, k, l, m, o, r, s,	-ug words b, d, g, j, l, m, n, p, r, s, t, u
king	cop	block	bug
ring	hop	dock	dug
sing	pop	lock	hug
wing	top	rock	jug
bring	chop	sock	mug
cling	drop	flock	rug
sting	chop	shock	tug
swing	shop	smock	plug
thing	stop	stock	snug
spring	mop	mock	slug

Phoneme Level Building Words Chart

a, h, m, t	a, h, m, p, t	a, h, m, n, p, t	a, b, c, d, h, m, n
at	am	an	an
mat	ham	pan	can
hat	hat	man	man
ham	pat	map	mad
	mat	mat	had
		hat	bad
		pat	

a, b, i, n, p, t	a, f, i, n, p, r, t	a, b, d, f, g, i, n, p, s, t	a, d, f, g, i, l, n, p, s, t
bit	fan	at	in
bat	ran	bat	pin
pat	pan	pat	fin
pan	pat	sat	fan
pin	pit	fat	fat
bin	pin	fit	fast
nip	fin	pit	last
	fi	pig	past
	fat	big	pat
	rat	rig	pan
	rap	rag	tan
	trap	drag	tin
		brag	tip

a, b, f, g, i, o, t, x	a, b, c, g, k, l, p, t, u	a, b, e, n, s, t	a, c, d, h, i, l, m, n, p, u
fig	bag	an	damp
big	bug	tan	kanp
bag	tug	ten	clamp
tag	tuck	set	champ
tax	luck	sent	chimp
fax	lack	net	chip
ax	back	nest	chin
ox	bat	best	inch
box	tab	bet	pinch
fox	cab	let	punch
fix	cap	lent	lunch

Children's Literature List with Multiple Rhyme Patterns

Benfanti, R. (2002). *Hide Clyde.* New York: Little Brown & Co.

Brown, M. W. (1989). *Goodnight moon.* New York: Scholastic.

Brown, M. W. (1999). *Another important book.* New York: Harper Collins.

Charlip, R. (1999). *Sleepytime rhyme.* New York: Greenwillow.

Degen, B. (1983). *Jamberry.* New York: Harper & Row.

Dodd, L. (1999). *Hairy Maclary and Zachary Quack.* Wellington, New Zealand.

DuQuette, K. (1999). *The house book.* New York: Putnam.

Ehlert, L. (2000). *Market day.* San Diego: Harcourt.

Fleming, D. (1991). *In the small, small pond.* New York: Holt, Rinehart, & Winston.

Fleming, D. (1991). *In the tall, tall grass.* New York: Holt, Rinehart, & Winston.

Fleming, D. (1994). *Barnyard banter.* New York: Holt, Rinehart, & Winston.

Fox, M. (2002). *The magic hat.* New York: Harcourt.

Gleman, R. G. (1979). *Hello, cat, you need a hat.* New York: Scholastic.

Hoberman, M. A. (1996). *One of each.* Boston: Little Brown.

Katz, M. J. (1990). *Ten potatoes in a pot.* New York: Harper & Row.

Kimmel, E. A. (1993). *The gingerbread man.* New York: Holiday House.

Langstaff, J. (1974). *Oh, a-hunting we will go.* New York: Atheneum.

Leopold, N. C., & Jeffers, S. (2002). *K is for kitten.* New York: Putnam.

Lewis, K., & Kirk, D. (1999). *Chugga chugga choo choo.* New York: Hyperion Books.

Lewis, K., & Kirk, D. (2002). *My truck is stuck.* New York: Hyperion Books.

Lowery, L. (1995). *Twist with a burger, jitter with a bug.* Boston: Houghton Mifflin.

Maccarone, G. (1992). *Itchy, itchy chicken pox.* New York: Scholastic.

Martin, B., & Archambault, J. (1991). *Chicka chicka boom boom.* New York: Simon & Schuster.

McPhail, D. (1993). *Pigs aplenty, pigs galore!* New York: Dutton.

Prelutsky, J. (2002). *The frogs wore red suspenders.* New York: Harper Collins.

Reid, B. (1999). *The party.* New York: Scholastic.

Shaw, N. (1986). *Sheep in a jeep.* Boston: Houghton Mifflin.

Shaw, N. (1989). *Sheep in a ship.* Boston: Houghton Mifflin.

Shaw, N. (1991). *Sheep in a shop.* Boston: Houghton Mifflin.

Shaw, N. (1992). *Sheep out to eat.* Boston: Houghton Mifflin.

Siomades, L. (2002). *Cuckoo can't find you.* Honesdale, PA: Boyds Mill Press.

Spohn, K. (2002). *The wet dry book.* New York: Random House.

Suen, A. (1998). *Window music.* New York: Viking.

Wadsworth, O. A. (2002). *Over in the meadow.* New York: North South Books.

Winthrop, E. (2001). *Dumpy La Rue.* New York: Holt, Rinehart, & Winston.

Yolen, J. (2000). *Off we go.* New York: Little Brown & Co.

Yolen, J. (2002). *Time for naps.* New York: Little Brown & Co.

Yolen, J., & Teague, M. (2000). *How do dinosaurs say goodnight?* New York: Blue Sky Press.

Elkonin Boxes with Two Phonemes

Elkonin Boxes with Three Phonemes

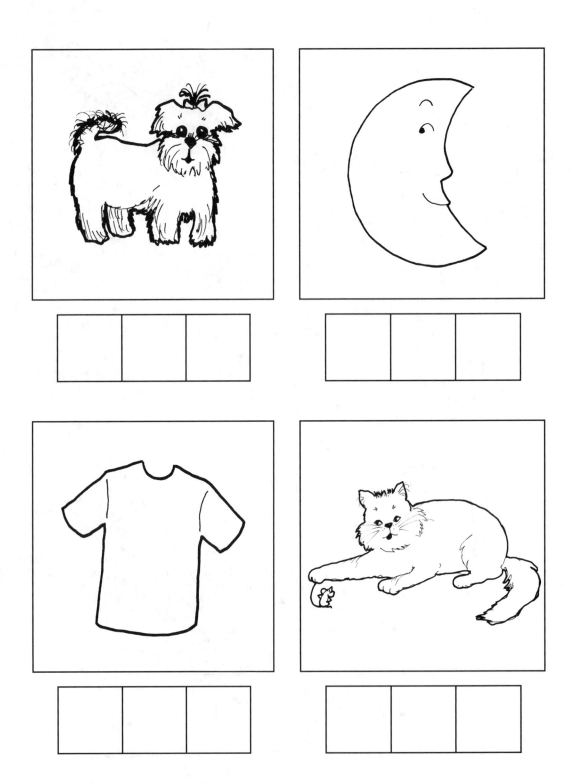

Appendix

Elkonin Boxes with Four Phonemes

Word Train Patterns

Appendix

Compound Words List

afternoon	baseball	bluegrass	carefree	dogcatcher
afterthought	baseboard	blueprint	carload	doghouse
aircraft	bathrobe	boardroom	carpool	dollhouse
airplane	bathroom	boathouse	cartwheel	doorbell
airport	bathtub	boatload	catfish	doorknob
anthill	battlefield	bobcat	catnip	doorman
anybody	beachcomber	bobtail	cattail	doorstep
anything	become	bookbag	chainsaw	doorstop
anywhere	bedbug	bookcase	chairman	doorway
applesauce	bedrock	bookend	chalkboard	downcast
armchair	bedroom	bookkeeper	checkerboard	downpour
armpit	bedspread	bookmark	cheeseburger	downspout
arrowhead	bedtime	bookmobile	classmate	downstairs
babysitter	beehive	bookshelf	classroom	downstream
backache	beekeeper	bookworm	clockwise	downtown
backbend	beeline	bottleneck	clothespin	dragonfly
backbone	beeswax	bowtie	cloudburst	driftwood
backdrop	bellhop	boxcar	cookbook	driveway
backfire	bellman	boyfriend	copycat	drumstick
background	bellyache	brainstorm	corkboard	dugout
backlash	benchmark	briefcase	corncob	eardrum
backpack	billboard	broadband	cornfield	earthquake
backslide	billfold	broadcast	cornhusker	earthworm
backstage	birdbath	Broadway	cornmeal	easygoing
backstop	birdhouse	broomstick	cornstarch	eggplant
backstretch	birdseed	bubblegum	countryside	eggshell
backstroke	birthday	buckeye	courthouse	elsewhere
backtalk	birthmark	bulldog	courtyard	evergreen
backup	birthplace	bulldozer	cowboy	everyday
backwash	birthstone	bullfrog	crosswalk	everything
backwoods	blackberry	bumblebee	crossword	everywhere
backyard	blackbird	busboy	cupcake	eyeball
ballroom	blackboard	buttercup	daybreak	eyebrow
bandwagon	blackmail	butterfly	daydream	eyeglasses
bareback	blacksmith	buttermilk	daylight	eyelash
barefoot	blockbuster	buttonhole	dayspring	eyelid
barnstorm	blueberry	candlestick	daytime	eyesight
barnyard	bluebird	cardboard	dishwasher	eyesore

eyewitness	ghostwriter	handwritten	housefly	lowercase
fairground	gingerbread	handyman	household	lunchbox
fairway	girlfriend	hangout	housekeeper	lunchroom
fanfare	goalkeeper	hardware	houseplant	lunchtime
farewell	goldfish	hardwood	housetop	mailbag
farmhand	goosebump	haystack	however	mailbox
farmhouse	grandchild	headache	icebox	mailman
feedback	granddaughter	headboard	income	mainframe
fencepost	grandfather	headdress	infield	mainland
fieldwork	grandmother	headfirst	ingrown	mainline
fingernail	grandparents	headgear	inland	mainstay
fingerprint	grandson	headlight	innkeeper	mastermind
firecracker	grandstand	headline	input	masterpiece
firefighter	grapefruit	headliner	inside	matchstick
firefly	grapevine	headphone	into	meadowlark
fireman	grasshopper	headquarters	itself	meanwhile
fireplace	graveyard	headstone	jackknife	meatball
fireproof	greenhouse	headstrong	jackpot	milkshake
fireside	gridlock	headway	jaybird	moonbeam
firewood	groundhog	heartburn	jaywalk	motorbike
fireworks	guideline	hedgehog	jellyfish	mousetrap
fishbowl	guideword	herself	jigsaw	mouthwash
fisherman	gumdrop	highland	keyboard	myself
flashback	gumshoe	highlight	keyhole	necktie
flashcard	hacksaw	highlighter	keynote	network
flashlight	hailstorm	highway	keystone	newscast
flowerpot	hairbrush	hillside	knapsack	newsletter
flyby	haircut	himself	ladybug	newspaper
football	hairdo	homecoming	lamppost	newsprint
foothills	hairdresser	homeland	lampshade	newsstand
foothold	hairstyle	homemade	landfall	newsworthy
footnote	halfback	homeowner	landfill	nightfall
footpath	hallmark	homeroom	landlady	nightgown
footprint	hallway	homesick	landlord	nightmare
footstep	hammerhead	homestretch	landmark	nightshirt
footstool	handbag	hometown	landscape	nighttime
footwork	handbook	homework	landslide	nobody
forecast	handcuff	honeymoon	letdown	noisemaker
forklift	handlebar	horseback	letup	northeast
fortnight	handout	horsefly	lifeboat	northwest
foxhole	handpick	horseplay	lifeguard	nosebleed
freeway	handrail	horsepower	lifelike	notebook
freshwater	handset	horseshoe	lifetime	nowhere
frogman	handshake	hourglass	lighthouse	oatmeal
frostbite	handspring	houseboat	linebacker	offspring
fruitcake	handstand	housebreak	lipstick	onlooker
gentleman	handwriting	housebroken	lookout	onto

otherwise	pigtail	rundown	sideways	stepladder
outbreak	pillbox	runoff	silverfish	stepmother
outburst	pinball	runway	silverware	stepsister
outcast	pincushion	sailboat	skateboard	stereotype
outcome	pipeline	sailfish	skyscraper	storefront
outcry	pitfall	salesman	snowball	storehouse
outdated	placemat	salesperson	snowdrift	storekeeper
outdoors	playground	saleswoman	snowflake	storeroom
outfit	playhouse	sandbox	snowman	storybook
outgoing	playmate	sandpaper	snowplow	storyline
outhouse	playoff	sandpiper	snowshoe	storyteller
outlaw	playpen	sandstorm	snowstorm	straightforward
outline	playroom	sawdust	softball	strawberry
outlook	playschool	scarecrow	softhearted	streamline
outpost	plaything	scrapbook	software	streetlight
output	playtime	seaboard	somebody	stronghold
outrage	plywood	seafood	someday	suitcase
outside	pocketbook	seahorse	somehow	summertime
outskirts	ponytail	seaman	someone	sunbathe
overall	popcorn	seaplane	someplace	sunburn
overalls	postcard	seaport	something	sundown
overcast	posthole	seashell	sometime	sunflower
overcoat	postmark	seashore	somewhat	sunrise
overcome	postmaster	seaside	somewhere	sunset
overhead	potbelly	seaweed	songwriter	sunshine
overheard	proofread	seaworthy	southeast	suntan
overkill	quarterback	setup	southwest	surfboard
overlap	quicksand	shadowbox	spacecraft	sweatshirt
overnight	racehorse	shipshape	spaceship	sweatshop
overrun	railroad	shipwreck	spacesuit	sweepstake
overseas	railway	shirttail	spearmint	sweetheart
oversees	rainbow	shoehorn	sportsman	swordfish
oversight	raincoat	shoelace	spotlight	tablecloth
overturn	raindrop	shoplift	springtime	tablespoon
overweight	rainfall	shortcake	stagecoach	tailgate
pancake	rainproof	shortcoming	staircase	tattletale
paperback	rainstorm	shortcut	stairway	teacup
paperclip	rainwater	shortfall	stairwell	teammate
paperweight	redhead	shorthanded	stakeout	teamwork
parkway	roadblock	shortsighted	stalemate	teapot
passerby	roadside	shortstop	starfish	teardrop
pathway	roadway	shotgun	starlight	teaspoon
peanut	roadwork	sidekick	steamboat	teatime
peppermint	roommate	sideline	steamroll	textbook
piggyback	rosebud	sidestep	steeplechase	Thanksgiving
piggybank	rowboat	sidetrack	stepbrother	thumbnail
pigpen	runaway	sidewalk	stepfather	thumbprint

thumbtack
tightrope
timeline
timetable
tiptoe
today
toenail
tombstone
tonight
toothbrush
toothpaste
toothpick
topnotch
torchlight
tossup
touchdown
trashcan
treehouse
trustworthy
tryout
tugboat
tumbleweeds
turnover
turnpike

turtleneck
typewriter
underdog
undermine
understand
underwear
upbeat
update
upgrade
uphill
uphold
upkeep
uplift
uppercase
upright
upright
uproar
uproot
upscale
upset
upstairs
upstream
upswing
uptight

uptown
viewpoint
volleyball
wallflower
wallpaper
warehouse
warehouse
warthog
washcloth
washstand
watchdog
watercolor
waterfall
waterfront
watermelon
waterproof
watertight
waterway
weatherman
weathervane
weekday
weekend
weeknight
whatever

wheelbarrow
wheelchair
whenever
wherever
whirlpool
whirlwind
whirlybird
whitewall
whoever
wholesale
widespread
wildcat
wildlife
willpower
windburn
windmill
windowpane
windowsill
windpipe
windshield
windstorm
wintergreen
wintertime
wisecrack

wishbone
withdraw
within
without
withstand
wonderland
woodchuck
woodpecker
woodwind
woodwork
workbench
workbook
workday
workout
worksheet
worthwhile
wristwatch
yardstick
yearbook
yourself
zookeeper

Syllable Word List

Words with One Syllable

ball	foal	hunt	lit	net	rang	skate	trot
barn	foot	hush	log	next	rap	skit	tub
bird	fork	hut	long	night	rash	slam	tug
board	four	jab	lost	nip	rat	slap	tusk
book	fox	jam	lot	nod	red	sleigh	two
boots	frog	jet	lox	not	rent	slim	van
bow	geese	jig	lump	nun	rest	snake	vault
boy	gift	job	lung	nut	rib	snap	vent
bus	girl	jog	mad	one	rich	snip	vest
can	goat	jug	man	pad	rid	stem	vet
cap	goose	junk	map	pan	rig	step	wag
cat	grapes	just	mask	pant	ring	stop	wax
chat	grip	keg	mast	pants	risk	sun	web
clock	gum	kept	mat	past	rob	swam	went
clown	had	key	math	pat	romp	swim	west
cow	ham	kid	melt	path	rub	swing	wet
crab	hand	king	men	peg	run	tab	whale
crop	hang	kit	mend	pen	rung	tack	whip
crown	has	kite	met	pest	rush	tag	wig
cup	hat	lamb	milk	pet	rust	tan	wind
dim	held	lamp	mink	pig	rut	tank	wing
dog	help	land	mint	pink	sad	tap	wink
drink	hem	lap	mist	pit	sag	tax	wish
drip	hen	last	mix	plop	sap	ten	with
drop	hex	led	mob	pod	sat	tent	won
drum	hint	leg	mom	pond	saw	test	wow
eight	hip	lend	moon	pop	seal	them	yak
fax	his	let	mop	pox	set	three	yam
feet	hit	lid	moth	pump	shark	tin	yank
fight	hog	lift	mouse	pup	sheep	tip	yelp
fin	honk	light	much	purse	shirt	tooth	yes
fish	horse	limp	mud	raft	shoe	top	yet
five	hot	link	mug	rag	shot	trap	zap
flag	house	lint	must	ram	shut	tree	zest
flip	hug	lip	nap	ramp	sit	trim	zip
flop	hum	list	nest	ran	six	trip	zoo

Words with Two Syllables

airport	commit	helmet	monkey	puppy	suitcase
apple	compact	hornet	monster	rabbit	support
baboon	cougar	igloo	morning	racquet	table
balloon	dolphin	jacket	mother	rapid	teacher
begin	donkey	jaguar	occur	rebel	tennis
brother	duckling	kitchen	panda	refer	tiger
bucket	elbow	kitten	paper	regret	toothbrush
buckle	expel	ladder	parrot	reindeer	transfer
camel	father	lemon	pencil	reptile	transmit
candle	flower	lesson	penguin	retail	tulip
candy	galley	letter	picnic	ribbon	turtle
carpet	gannet	lion	porpoise	scissors	water
chicken	Georgia	lobster	preferred	shoulder	window
coffee	giraffe	mammal	present	sister	
comet	gosling	midnight	propel	soccer	
comment	hammer	mittens	puffin	submit	

Words with Three Syllables

addition	cavalier	everyone	masterpiece	policeman
aerobic	cheeseburger	excellent	mathematics	principal
afternoon	coffeepot	exercise	microscope	quarterback
angelic	commitment	flamingo	monarchy	rattlesnake
animal	committee	forever	multiple	scenery
anyone	companion	furniture	multiply	separate
anything	computer	gallery	mystery	September
anytime	concentrate	gingerbread	Nintendo	skeleton
anywhere	cosmonaut	granddaughter	November	sombrero
appetite	crocodile	grandfather	nursery	sorcery
assistant	December	grandmother	occasion	subtraction
asteroid	departing	gymnastics	octagon	summertime
astronaut	dinosaur	hamburger	October	supplement
banana	disaster	happiness	overcast	syndicate
basketball	discrepant	hexagon	overcoat	telephone
bicycle	division	however	overcome	telescope
bubblegum	duplicate	hurricane	overflow	Thanksgiving
buccaneer	dynamic	ignorant	overlook	tornado
buffalo	elephant	important	overture	transgression
buttercup	elevate	Indian	overview	treachery
butterfly	embankment	interstate	parakeet	tricycle
buttermilk	embarking	ladybug	patriot	undergo
butternut	envelope	library	pentagon	underground
butterscotch	equipment	linebacker	permitted	understand
candlestick	everyday	lioness	piano	violin

Words with Four Syllables

activity
alligator
amphibian
anybody
approachable
architecture
arithmetic
astronomy
biography
calculator
calligraphy
choreograph
compatible
concentration
contribution
conversation

democracy
democratic
discrepancy
elevator
escalator
everybody
exceptional
expandable
fashionable
favorable
February
graduation
helicopter
implication
information
information

January
machinery
magnificent
merry-go-round
motorcycle
multipurpose
occupation
operator
presentation
professional
punishable
questionable
remarkable
rhinoceros
rigidity
secretary

stationery
systematic
taxidermy
television
transportable
understanding
underwater
unicycle
universal
upholstery
utility
watercolor
watermelon

Words with Five or More Syllables

acceptability
accountability
adaptability
anniversary
authenticity
autobiography
chronological
cinematography
classification
complimentary
cosmopolitan

documentation
economical
elementary
eligibility
explanatory
hippopotamus
hospitality
identification
impossibility
international
justification

legibility
Louisiana
meteorologist
metropolitan
multiplication
notification
observatory
pediatrician
personality
personification
preliminary

refrigerator
reliability
responsibility
revolutionary
rudimentary
supplementary
visibility
vocabulary
vocalization

Phonogram List

Phonograms That Begin with 'a'

-ab	-ace	-ack	-act	-ad
blab	ace	back	act	bad
cab	brace	black	fact	clad
crab	face	clack	pact	dad
dab	grace	crack	tact	fad
drab	lace	flack	tract	glad
grab	mace	hack		had
jab	pace	jack		lad
lab	place	knack		mad
nab	race	lack		pad
scab	space	pack		sad
slab	trace	quack		tad
tab		rack		
		sack		
		shack		
		slack		
		smack		
		snack		
		stack		
		tack		
		track		
		whack		

-ade	-aft	-ag	-age	-aid
bade	craft	brag	age	aid
blade	draft	crag	cage	braid
fade	graft	drag	gage	laid
glade	raft	flag	page	maid
grade	shaft	gag	rage	paid
jade	waft	hag	sage	raid
made		jag	stage	staid
shade		lag	wage	
spade		nag		
trade		rag		
wade		sag		
		slag		
		snag		
		stag		
		swag		
		tag		
		wag		

-ail	-ain	-aint	-air	-ake
ail	brain	faint	air	bake
bail	chain	paint	chair	brake
fail	drain	quaint	fair	cake
flail	gain	saint	flair	drake
frail	grain	taint	hair	fake
hail	lain		lair	flake
jail	main		pair	lake
mail	pain		stair	make
nail	plain			quake
pail	rain			rake
quail	slain			sake
rail	Spain			shake
sail	sprain			snake
snail	stain			stake
tail	strain			take
trail	swain			wake
wail	train			
	twain			
	vain			

-ale	-alk	-all	-am	-ame
bale	balk	all	am	blame
dale	calk	ball	cam	came
gale	chalk	call	clam	dame
hale	stalk	fall	cram	fame
kale	talk	gall	dam	flame
male	walk	hall	dram	frame
pale		mall	gram	game
sale		pall	ham	lame
scale		small	jam	name
shale		squall	ram	same
stale		stall	scam	shame
tale		tall	scram	tame
wale		wall	sham	
whale			slam	
			swam	
			tam	
			tram	
			yam	

-amp	-an	-ance	-anch	-and
amp	an	chance	blanch	and
camp	ban	dance	branch	band
champ	bran	France	ranch	bland
clamp	can	glance	stanch	brand
cramp	clan	lance		gland
damp	Dan	prance		grand
lamp	fan	stance		hand
ramp	flan	trance		land
scamp	Jan			sand
stamp	man			stand
tamp	pan			strand
tramp	plan			
vamp	ran			
	scan			
	span			
	tan			
	than			
	van			

-ane	-ang	-ank	-ant	-ap
bane	bang	bank	ant	cap
cane	clang	blank	can't	chap
crane	fang	clank	chant	clap
lane	gang	crank	grant	dap
mane	hang	dank	pant	flap
pane	pang	drank	plant	gap
plane	rang	flank	rant	lap
sane	sang	frank	scant	map
vane	slang	hank	slant	nap
wane	sprang	lank		pap
	tang	plank		rap
	twang	prank		sap
		rank		scrap
		sank		slap
		shank		snap
		shrank		strap
		spank		tap
		stank		trap
		swank		wrap
		tank		yap
		thank		zap
		yank		

-ape	-ar	-ard	-are	-ark
ape	bar	bard	bare	bark
cape	car	card	blare	dark
drape	char	guard	care	hark
gape	far	hard	dare	lark
grape	jar	lard	fare	mark
nape	mar	shard	flare	park
scrape	par	yard	glare	shark
shape	scar		hare	spark
tape	spar		mare	stark
	star		pare	
	tar		rare	
			scare	
			share	
			snare	
			spare	
			square	
			stare	
			ware	

-arm	-art	-ash	-ask	-asp
alarm	art	ash	ask	clasp
arm	cart	bash	cask	gasp
charm	chart	brash	flask	grasp
farm	dart	cash	mask	hasp
harm	mart	clash	task	rasp
	part	crash		
	smart	dash		
	start	flash		
	tart	gash		
		gnash		
		hash		
		lash		
		mash		
		rash		
		sash		
		slash		
		smash		
		splash		
		stash		
		thrash		
		trash		

-ass	-ast	-aste	-at	-atch
bass	blast	baste	at	batch
brass	cast	taste	bat	catch
class	fast	haste	brat	hatch
glass	last	paste	cat	latch
grass	mast		chat	match
lass	past		fat	patch
mass	vast		flat	scratch
pass			gnat	thatch
			hat	
			mat	
			pat	
			rat	
			sat	
			tat	
			that	
			vat	

-ate	-ath	-ave	-aw	-ax
ate	bath	brave	aw	ax
crate	lath	cave	caw	fax
date	math	crave	claw	flax
fate	path	gave	craw	lax
gate	wrath	grave	draw	max
grate		pave	flaw	sax
hate		rave	gnaw	tax
late		save	haw	wax
mate		shave	jaw	
plate		slave	law	
rate		stave	maw	
skate		wave	paw	
slate			raw	
state			saw	
			slaw	
			squaw	
			straw	
			taw	
			thaw	
			yaw	

-ay
bay
bray
cray
day
flay
fray
gay
gray
hay
jay
lay
may
nay
pay
play
pray
quay
ray
say
slay
spay
splay
spray
stay
stray
sway
tray
way

Phonograms That Begin with 'e'

-each	-ead	-ead	-eak	-eal
beach	bread	bead	beak	deal
bleach	dead	knead	bleak	heal
breach	dread	lead	creak	meal
each	head	mead	freak	peal
leach	lead	read	leak	real
peach	read		peak	seal
preach	spread		sneak	squeal
reach	thread		speak	steal
teach	tread		squeak	teal
			streak	veal
			teak	zeal
			tweak	
			weak	

-eam	-ean	-ear	-east	-eat
beam	bean	clear	beast	beat
cream	clean	dear	east	bleat
dream	dean	ear	feast	cheat
gleam	glean	fear	least	cleat
ream	lean	gear	yeast	eat
scream	mean	hear		feat
seam	wean	near		heat
steam		rear		meat
stream		sear		neat
team		shear		peat
		smear		pleat
		spear		seat
		tear		teat
		year		treat
				wheat

-eck	-ed	-ee	-eed	-eek
check	bed	bee	bleed	cheek
deck	bled	fee	breed	creek
fleck	bred	flee	creed	Greek
heck	fed	free	deed	leek
neck	fled	glee	feed	meek
peck	led	knee	freed	peek
speck	red	lee	greed	reek
wreck	shed	see	heed	seek
	shred	spree	kneed	sleek
	sled	tee	need	week
	sped	tree	reed	
	wed	wee	seed	
			speed	
			steed	
			tweed	
			weed	

-eel	-een	-eep	-eer	-eet
creel	green	beep	beer	beet
eel	keen	cheep	deer	feet
feel	preen	creep	jeer	fleet
heel	queen	deep	leer	greet
keel	screen	jeep	peer	meet
kneel	seen	keep	queer	sheet
peel	sheen	peep	seer	skeet
reel	spleen	seep	sneer	sleet
steel	teen	sheep	steer	street
wheel		sleep		sweet
		steep		tweet
		sweep		
		weep		

-eg	-ell	-elt	-en	-end
beg	bell	belt	den	bend
dreg	cell	dwelt	glen	blend
Greg	dell	felt	hen	end
keg	fell	knelt	men	fend
leg	jell	melt	pen	lend
meg	knell	pelt	ten	mend
peg	quell	smelt	then	rend
	sell	welt	when	send
	shell		wren	spend
	smell		yen	tend
	spell			trend
	swell			vend
	tell			wend
	well			
	yell			

-ent	-ess	-est	-et	-ew
bent	bless	best	bet	blew
cent	chess	chest	fret	brew
dent	dress	crest	get	chew
gent	less	fest	jet	crew
lent	mess	guest	let	dew
rent	press	jest	met	drew
scent	stress	nest	net	few
sent	tress	pest	pet	flew
spent		quest	set	hew
tent		rest	wet	knew
vent		test	whet	new
went		vest	yet	pew
		west		screw
		zest		stew
				threw

Phonograms That Begin with 'i'

-ice	-ick	-id	-ide	-ift
dice	brick	bid	bide	drift
ice	chick	did	bride	gift
lice	click	grid	chide	lift
mice	crick	hid	glide	rift
nice	flick	id	hide	shift
price	hick	kid	pride	sift
rice	kick	lid	ride	swift
slice	lick	mid	side	thrift
spice	nick	quid	slide	
splice	pick	rid	snide	
thrice	prick	skid	stride	
trice	quick	slid	tide	
twice	sick	squid	wide	
vice	slick			
	stick			
	thick			
	tick			
	trick			
	wick			

-ig	-ight	-ike	-ile	-ill
big	blight	bike	bile	bill
dig	bright	dike	file	chill
fig	fight	hike	mile	dill
gig	flight	like	pile	drill
jig	fright	Mike	smile	fill
pig	knight	pike	stile	frill
rig	light	spike	tile	gill
sprig	might	strike	vile	grill
swig	night		while	hill
twig	plight			ill
wig	right			kill
	sight			mill
	slight			pill
	tight			quill
				shrill
				sill
				skill
				spill
				still
				thrill
				till
				will

-im	-ime	-in	-ind	-ine
brim	chime	bin	bind	brine
dim	clime	chin	blind	dine
grim	crime	din	find	fine
him	dime	fin	grind	line
prim	grime	gin	hind	mine
rim	lime	grin	kind	nine
slim	mime	kin	mind	pine
swim	prime	pin	rind	shine
trim	slime	shin	wind	shrine
vim	time	sin		spine
whim		skin		swine
		spin		thine
		thin		tine
		tin		vine
		twin		whine
		win		wine

-ing	-ink	-int	-ip	-ipe
bring	blink	glint	blip	gripe
cling	brink	hint	chip	pipe
ding	chink	lint	clip	ripe
fling	clink	mint	dip	snipe
king	drink	print	drip	stripe
ping	fink	splint	flip	swipe
ring	ink	sprint	grip	tripe
sing	kink	squint	hip	wipe
sling	link	stint	kip	
spring	mink	tint	lip	
sting	pink		nip	
string	rink		pip	
swing	shrink		quip	
thing	sink		rip	
wing	slink		ship	
wring	stink		sip	
zing	think		skip	
	wink		slip	
			snip	
			strip	
			tip	
			trip	
			whip	
			zip	

-it	-ite	-ive	-ix
bit	bite	chive	fix
fit	kite	dive	mix
flit	mite	drive	nix
grit	quite	five	six
hit	rite	hive	
kit	site	jive	
knit	sprite	live	
lit	white	strive	
pit	write	thrive	
quit			
sit			
skit			
slit			
spit			
split			
twit			
wit			

Phonograms That Begin with 'o'

-oat	-oak	-ob	-ock	-od
bloat	cloak	blob	block	clod
boat	croak	cob	chock	cod
coat	oak	fob	clock	mod
float	soak	glob	cock	nod
goat		gob	crock	plod
gloat		job	dock	pod
moat		knob	flock	prod
oat		lob	frock	rod
		mob	hock	shod
		rob	jock	sod
		slob	knock	trod
		snob	lock	
		sob	mock	
			pock	
			rock	
			shock	
			smock	
			sock	
			stock	
			tock	

-og	-oil	-oke	-old	-ole
bog	boil	bloke	bold	dole
clog	broil	broke	cold	hole
cog	coil	choke	fold	mole
dog	foil	coke	gold	pole
flog	oil	joke	hold	role
fog	soil	poke	mold	sole
frog	spoil	smoke	old	stole
grog	toil	spoke	scold	whole
hog		stoke	sold	
jog		stroke	told	
log		woke		
slog		yoke		
smog				
tog				

-oll	-one	-ood	-ook	-ool
droll	bone	good	book	cool
knoll	clone	hood	brook	drool
poll	cone	stood	cook	fool
roll	crone	wood	crook	pool
scroll	drone		hook	school
stroll	hone		look	spool
toll	lone		nook	stool
troll	phone		shook	tool
	prone		took	
	shone			
	stone			
	tone			
	zone			

-oom	-oon	-oop	-oot	-op
bloom	croon	coop	boot	bop
boom	loon	droop	hoot	chop
broom	moon	hoop	loot	cop
doom	noon	loop	moot	crop
gloom	soon	scoop	root	drop
groom	spoon	sloop	scoot	flop
loom	swoon	snoop	shoot	fop
room		stoop	toot	glop
zoom		swoop		hop
		troop		lop
				mop
				plop
				pop
				prop
				shop
				slop
				sop
				stop
				top

-ope	-ore	-orn	-ose	-ot
cope	bore	born	chose	blot
grope	chore	corn	close	clot
hope	core	horn	hose	cot
lope	fore	morn	nose	dot
mope	more	scorn	pose	got
nope	pore	shorn	prose	hot
pope	score	sworn	rose	jot
rope	shore	thorn	those	knot
scope	snore	worn		lot
slope	sore			not
	spore			plot
	store			pot
	swore			rot
	tore			shot
	wore			slot
				snot
				spot
				tot
				trot

-ound	-ouse	-out	-ow	-ow
bound	blouse	bout	blow	bow
found	douse	clout	bow	brow
ground	grouse	flout	crow	chow
hound	house	gout	flow	cow
mound	mouse	grout	glow	how
pound	rouse	lout	grow	now
round	souse	out	know	plow
sound	spouse	pout	low	prow
wound		scout	mow	row
		shout	row	scow
		snout	show	sow
		spout	slow	vow
		sprout	snow	
		stout	sow	
		tout	stow	
		trout	tow	

-own	-own	-ox	-oy
brown	blown	box	boy
clown	flown	fox	coy
crown	grown	lox	joy
down	known	pox	Roy
drown	mown		soy
gown	shown		toy
town	sown		ploy
	thrown		

Phonograms That Begin with 'u'

-ub	-uck	-ud	-udge	-ue
club	Buck	bud	budge	blue
cub	chuck	cud	drudge	clue
drub	cluck	dud	fudge	cue
dub	duck	mud	grudge	due
flub	luck	spud	judge	flue
grub	muck	stud	nudge	glue
hub	pluck	thud	sludge	hue
nub	puck		smudge	true
pub	shuck		trudge	
rub	snuck			
scrub	struck			
shrub	stuck			
snub	suck			
stub	truck			
sub	tuck			
tub				

-uff	-ug	-um	-ump	-un
bluff	bug	bum	bump	bun
buff	chug	chum	chump	fun
cuff	drug	drum	clump	gun
fluff	dug	glum	dump	nun
gruff	hug	gum	frump	pun
huff	jug	hum	grump	run
puff	mug	mum	hump	shun
ruff	plug	plum	jump	spun
scuff	pug	rum	lump	stun
snuff	rug	scum	plump	sun
stuff	shrug	slum	pump	
	slug	strum	rump	
	smug	sum	slump	
	snug	swum	stump	
	thug		sump	
	tug		thump	
			trump	

-unch	-ung	-unk	-unt	-ush
brunch	clung	bunk	blunt	blush
bunch	hung	chunk	bunt	brush
crunch	lung	clunk	grunt	crush
hunch	rung	drunk	hunt	flush
lunch	slung	dunk	punt	gush
munch	sprung	flunk	runt	hush
punch	stung	funk	shunt	lush
	sung	hunk	stunt	mush
	swung	junk		plush
	wrung	plunk		rush
		punk		slush
		shrunk		thrush
		skunk		
		slunk		
		spunk		
		stunk		
		sunk		
		trunk		

-ust	-ut
bust	but
crust	cut
dust	glut
gust	gut
just	hut
must	jut
rust	nut
thrust	rut
trust	shut
	smut
	strut

Robbie the Robot: Script for Lesson #1

Instructor: (Advance Organizer) **You've already learned about the sounds of letters. Today, you are going to learn how to work with the sounds in some special ways. You will learn how to put sounds together to make words. You will also learn how to take apart a word and say it sound-by-sound. Learning these things can help you become a good reader in first grade.**

Is everybody ready to learn some special things about sounds?

Students: (*affirmative response*)

Instructor: **Good! Let's get started.**

The first thing we need to do is meet a new friend who will be helping us to learn more about sounds. (Show students the picture of Robbie the Robot.) **Everybody, say hello to Robbie the Robot!**

Students: *Hello, Robbie!*

Instructor: (Look at Robbie as if you are waiting for a response and then realize your "mistake.") **Uh oh! I forgot to tell you something. Robbie can't understand us when we talk like we usually do. He can only say or understand words one sound at a time. If we want to say "Hello, Robbie," we must say it one sound at a time so that he can understand us.**

Listen, I'll show you how. H-e-ll-o, R-o-bb-ie.
(In a Robbie-the-Robot voice, respond) **H-e-ll-o!**
Now let's all say "Hello" to Robbie again, but this time let's say it sound-by-sound.

Instructor & Students: ***H-e-ll-o, R-o-bb-ie!*** (prompt students who are having difficulty segmenting the sounds)

Instructor: (In a Robbie-the-Robot voice, respond) **H-e-ll-o!**

That was much better. That time Robbie understood what we were saying.

Sometimes it's hard to tell where to break a word apart to say it sound-by-sound, but we will be getting much better at it in the next few days.

Now, Robbie will say some words to you. Remember that he will say the words sound-by-sound. I want you to tell me what words he says. Are you ready to listen very carefully?

Students: (*affirmative response*)

Instructor: **Good. Let's get started. Listen to the sounds Robbie says, then say the whole word.**

(Say each segmented word—across each row—in a Robbie voice and wait for students to blend the phonemes and to say the whole word. Provide praise and corrective feedback as needed. Be sure that each student says each word correctly before moving on to the next word.)

a-t	i-f	g-o	t-o	ou-t	o-n
s-u-n	f-a-n	v-e-t	m-o-p	s-a-t	r-o-b

Terrific job! You figured out every word that Robbie said. Now, let's say some words sound-by-sound so that Robbie can understand what we are saying. Are you ready to say some words sound-by-sound?

Students: (*affirmative response*)

Instructor: **Good! Let's get started. I'll tell you the word and you say it sound-by-sound so that Robbie can understand.**

(Say each word and direct students to say the word sound-by-sound. Provide praise and corrective feedback as needed. Ensure that each student is able to segment each word correctly before moving on to the next word. When you detect an error, use the model, lead, test, retest procedure.)

at	if	go	to	out	on
sun	fan	vet	mop	sat	rob

That was terrific! Robbie could understand every one of those words when you said them sound-by-sound.

Let's review what we've learned. I'll call on you one at a time to blend some sounds together to make a word. (Ask individual students to blend the following words.)

s-o	r-u-n	l-i-p	s-a-t	f-i-n	m-u-d

Now, I'll call on you one at a time to say a word sound-by-sound. (Ask individual students to segment the following words.)

fan	mop	rat	sip	fat	rub

Robbie the Robot: Script for Lesson #2

Instructor: **Today, we are going to practice blending sounds together and taking them apart just like we did before. Remember that when we speak to Robbie the Robot, we must say the words sound-by-sound. When Robbie speaks to us, he'll say the words sound-by-sound and we need to blend them together to get words that we can understand. We'll start by saying some of the same words that we said last time. Is everybody ready?**

Students: (*affirmative response*)

Instructor: **Good. Let's get started. Listen to the sounds that Robbie will say and tell me what words they make.**

(Say each segmented word in a Robbie voice and wait for students to blend the phonemes and to say the whole word. Provide praise and corrective feedback as needed. Use the model, lead, test, retest procedure as needed.)

a-t	i-f	g-o	t-o	ou-t	o-n
s-u-n	f-a-n	v-e-t	m-o-p	s-a-t	r-o-b
m-a-d	f-u-n	b-a-t	r-a-p	c-u-p	m-u-d

Terrific job! You remembered how to figure out words that Robbie says. You even figured out some longer words. Now, let's practice saying some words sound-by-sound so that Robbie can understand what we are saying. Are you ready to say the words sound-by-sound?

Students: (*affirmative response*)

Instructor: **Good! Let's get started. Remember, I'll tell you the word and you say it sound-by-sound so that Robbie can understand.**

(Say each word and direct students to say the word sound-by-sound. Provide praise and corrective feedback as needed. Ensure that each student is able to segment each word correctly before moving on to the next word.)

at	if	go	do	out	on
sun	fin	met	mop	fat	rob
mad	fun	sat	rap	cut	pup

That was terrific! Robbie could understand every one of those words when you said them sound-by-sound. You're getting really good at saying words sound-by-sound and blending sounds together to make a word. Now we're going to practice using some even longer words. Do you think you can figure out some long words?

Students: (*affirmative response*)

Instructor: **Good. Let's get started. First Robbie will say some long words for you to figure out. Listen and blend the sounds together.**

(Say each segmented word in a Robbie voice and wait for students to blend the phonemes and to say the whole word. Provide praise and corrective feedback as needed.)

t-ea-ch-er	p-i-tch-er
h-o-pp-ing	j-u-m-p-r-o-pe

Boy, that was tough work! It's hard to remember all of those sounds. The best way to remember is to blend the parts together as you go. I'll show you.

For example, when I heard Robbie say "teacher," I started blending sounds together in my head right away. He said "t-ea," and right away in my head I said "tea." Then when Robbie said the "ch" sound, I added it to the "tea" in my head and I got "teach." When he said the "er' sound, it was easy for me to add it to "teach" to get "teacher."

Let's try some more long words and see if you can blend the sounds together in your head as we go. Listen.

r-o-ck-e-t

What word? (Wait for student responses.) **Did you blend the sounds together in your head? Did you say "ro," and then "rock," and then "rocket"? Good! Let's try some more.**

n-o-te-b-oo-k	s-l-i-pp-er-y
r-u-nn-er-s	t-o-g-e-th-er

You're doing a terrific job blending sounds together. Now let's see if you can say some long words sound-by-sound so that Robbie can understand them. Listen.

(Say each word and direct students to say the word sound-by-sound. Provide praise and corrective feedback as needed. Ensure that each student is able to segment each word correctly before moving on to the next word.)

little	kitten	sleepy
farmer	student	animal

You've done a terrific job blending and taking apart some long words. Next time we'll be talking to Robbie and he'll be talking to us.

Robbie the Robot: Script for Lesson #3

Instructor: **Today, we are going to practice blending sounds together and taking them apart just like we did before. Remember that when we speak to Robbie the Robot, we must say the words sound-by-sound. When Robbie speaks to us, he'll say the words sound-by-sound and we need to blend them together to get words that we can understand. We'll start by saying some of the same words that we said last time. Is everybody ready?**

Students: (*affirmative response*)

Instructor: **Good. Let's get started. Listen to the sounds that Robbie will say and tell me what words they make.**

(Say each segmented word in a Robbie voice and wait for students to blend the phonemes and to say the whole word. Provide praise and corrective feedback as needed. Use the model, lead, test, retest procedure as needed.)

i-t	i-n	g-o	p-ie	ou-t	o-n
b-u-n	t-a-n	m-e-t	t-o-p	r-a-t	r-o-ck
s-a-d	s-u-n	h-a-t	n-a-p	p-i-t	l-i-d
b-e-s-t	c-l-i-p	s-n-a-ke	j-u-m-p	l-a-s-t	d-i-s-k

Terrific job! You remembered how to figure out words that Robbie says. You even figured out some longer words. Now, let's practice saying some words sound-by-sound so that Robbie can understand what we are saying. Are you ready to say the words sound-by-sound?

Students: (*affirmative response*)

Instructor: **Good! Let's get started. Remember, I'll tell you the word and you say it sound-by-sound so that Robbie can understand.**

(Say each word and direct students to say the word sound-by-sound. Provide praise and corrective feedback as needed. Ensure that each student is able to segment each word correctly before moving on to the next word.)

up	it	ice	to	egg	tie
run	fin	set	hop	cat	rib
mud	win	cot	rap	vat	pup
most	snip	flake	limp	smoke	lift

That was terrific! Robbie could understand every one of those words when you said them sound-by-sound. You're getting really good at saying words sound-by-sound and blending sounds together to make a word. Now we're going to practice using some even longer words. Are you ready for more long words like the ones we did yesterday?

Students: (*affirmative response*)

Instructor: **Good. Let's get started. First Robbie will say some long words for you to figure out. Listen and blend the sounds together.**

(Say each segmented word in a Robbie voice and wait for students to blend the phonemes and to say the whole word. Provide praise and corrective feedback as needed.)

s-ai-l-or	f-i-sh-ing
h-o-pp-ing	m-o-th-er

Boy, that was tough work! It's hard to remember all of those sounds. The best way to remember is to blend the parts together as you go.

For example, when I heard Robbie say "sailor," I started blending sounds together in my head right away. He said "s-ai," and, right away, in my head I said "sai." Then when Robbie said the "l" sound, I added it to the "sai" in my head and I got "sail." When he said the "or" sound, it was easy for me to add it to "sail" to get "sailor."

Let's try some more long words and see if you can blend the sounds together in your head as we go. Listen.

f-a-s-t-er

What word? (Wait for student responses.) **Did you blend the sounds together in your head? Did you say 'fa,' and then 'fas,' and then 'fast,' and then 'faster'? Good! Let's try some more.**

c-r-o-c-o-d-i-le	t-oa-s-t-er
p-i-c-n-i-c	b-a-s-k-e-t

You're doing a terrific job blending sounds together. Now let's see if you can say some long words sound-by-sound so that Robbie can understand them. Listen.

(Say each word and direct students to say the word sound-by-sound. Provide praise and corrective feedback as needed. Ensure that each student is able to segment each word correctly before moving on to the next word.)

puppy	pocket	giraffe
table	slowest	rainbow

You've done a terrific job blending and taking apart some long words. Next time we'll be talking to Robbie and he'll be talking to us.

Robbie the Robot: Script for Lesson #4

Instructor: So far we have learned how to blend sounds together to make a word and how to break words apart and say them sound-by-sound. We blended and took apart short words and long words. Today we are going to practice these new skills and use them to talk with Robbie the Robot.

Let's begin by practicing blending some of Robbie's sounds together to make words. Is everybody ready to blend sounds?

Students: (*affirmative response*)

Instructor: **Good. Let's get started. Listen to the sounds that Robbie says and tell me what words they make.**

(Say each segmented word in a Robbie voice and wait for students to blend the phonemes and to say the whole word. Provide praise and corrective feedback as needed. Use the model, lead, test, retest procedure as needed.)

a-t	i-t	g-o	d-o	ou-t	o-n
f-u-n	r-a-n	m-e-t	h-o-p	s-a-t	r-o-b
b-a-d	d-u-ck	c-a-t	n-a-p	c-u-p	m-u-d
l-a-s-t	f-l-i-p	t-r-ai-n	d-a-m-p	m-o-s-t	r-e-s-t

Good job! Let's do some longer words. Remember to blend the sounds together in your head as Robbie says them.

r-a-d-i-o   s-w-ea-t-er   f-i-n-i-sh   t-e-l-e-ph-o-ne

Wow! You did a great job blending all those sounds together to make words. Did you remember to blend the sounds together in your head?

Students: (*affirmative response*)

Instructor: **Good! Now I will give each of you some words to say to Robbie sound-by-sound. Remember to break the words apart and say only one sound at a time.** (Say each word and direct individual students to say the word sound-by-sound. Provide praise and corrective feedback as needed.)

at	if	go	do	out	on
sun	fin	met	mop	fat	rob
mad	fun	sat	rap	cut	pup
fast	slip	brake	lamp	cost	desk

That was terrific! Robbie could understand every one of those words when you said them sound-by-sound.

Now I want you to talk with Robbie. You'll need to listen carefully to him and blend the sounds he says to make words. Remember that when you talk to him, you must say each word sound-by-sound so that he can understand you. Are you ready? Good.

(In a "Robbie" voice, ask each student questions, such as those below, saying each word sound-by-sound. Prompt students, if needed, to respond to Robbie by saying their words sound-by-sound.)

Wh-a-t i-s y-ou-r n-a-me?

H-ow o-l-d are y-ou?

D-o y-ou h-a-ve a-n-y b-r-o-th-er-s or s-i-s-t-er-s? (etc.)

(Continue the sound-by-sound conversation for the remainder of the session.)

Wow! You have done a wonderful job talking with Robbie so that he could understand you. You have learned how to blend words and take words apart very well.

Robbie the Robot: Script for Lessons 5–13
General Directions

For each lesson, the passage will be read a total of four times. For the first time, the instructor should model fluent reading of the passage. To do this, read aloud to the group while you point to each word.

For the second reading of the passage, you should guide the group in reading the passage along with you using echo reading. In echo reading, the instructor reads one line of text while pointing to each word. The students then read the same line of text while the instructor points to the words again. Continue with this process through the passage, one line at a time.

The third reading of the passage should be a choral reading. In choral reading, the instructor and students read through the entire passage together. This reading should be as fluent as possible. Additional practice reading the passage may be appropriate with some students.

After three readings of the passage, ask the students to help you find words in the passage that have the target sound (each passage has an accompanying list of target words). Write each word they find on paper. Practice the phonological awareness activities with each set of words as detailed in the lesson script.

Finally, read the passage with the students a fourth time. During this reading, the students should stop to segment and blend those words with the target sound. Be certain to make *explicit the connection between the phonological awareness tasks and the passage reading.*

Lesson Script

Instructor: **Today we are going to practice reading a passage and using some of the skills we have already learned. I want you to listen to me read and follow along with your eyes.**

(Read passage and point to each word.)

This time, I'd like for you to read the passage along with me. First, look and listen while I read a sentence. Then you read the sentence with me. Everybody ready?

(Read the passage again, still pointing to each word. Read each sentence twice, once as a model then once as the students read with you—echo reading.)

That was terrific! Let's read it one more time, this time let's all read together. Ready?

(Read the passage a third time with students reading along throughout the passage—choral reading.)

Good reading! Now I'd like for you to help me look at the words in this passage. Help me find all the words that have a (say target sound) in them. I'll write down each word that we find.

(Assist students in finding all words with the target sound and write them down.)

Great! Now, let's practice saying these words with Robbie. Robbie will say a word and you see if you can figure out what word he says.

(Say each of the words sound-by-sound in a Robbie the Robot voice as students blend the sounds to say the word.)

Now you get to say the words sound-by-sound so that Robbie can understand them.

(Guide the group in saying each word sound-by-sound. Then ask individual students to practice segmenting each word.)

That was good! Now we are going to read our passage one more time. This time, when we come to one of the words with the (say target sound) sound, we'll say it sound-by-sound and then say the whole word.

(Read the passage with the students. At each word with the target sound, stop and guide the students in saying the word sound-by-sound and blended. Do not spend time correcting students' errors during the passage reading. Let your reading serve as a model.)

Good reading! Remember, when you are reading, that you can say a word sound-by-sound to figure out the word. Then, you can blend the sounds together to make the whole word.

Robbie the Robot: Script for Lessons 14–18
General Directions

This phase of the intervention is similar to the last phase. The passage reading portion is exactly the same. The difference is that the last five passages highlight vowels for target sounds. The activities with the sounds are, therefore, somewhat different.

For each lesson, you will continue to read the passage three times (modeling, echo reading, then choral reading), ask the students to help you find words that have the target sound, write each word, practice the phonological awareness activities with each set of words, and read the passage again together.

Some students may need additional practice with the concept of rhyming. Such practice may be incorporated into these lessons by spending additional time generating rhyme examples with students.

Throughout the lesson, remember to make *explicit the connection between the phonological awareness tasks and the passage reading.*

Lesson Script

Instructor: **Today we are going to practice reading a passage and then we're going to do some new activities. First, I want you to listen to me read and follow along with your eyes.**

(Read passage and point to each word.)

This time, I'd like for you to read the passage along with me. First, look and listen while I read a sentence. Then you read the sentence with me.

(Read the passage again, still pointing to each word. Read each sentence twice, once as a model then once as the students read with you—echo reading.)

That was terrific! Let's read it one more time, this time let's all read together. Ready?

(Read the passage a third time with students reading along throughout the passage—choral reading.)

Good reading! Now I'd like for you to help me look at the words in this passage. Help me find all the words that have a (say target sound) in them. I'll write down each word that we find.

(Assist students in finding all words with the target sound and write them down.)

Great! Now, let's try to find as many words as we can that rhyme with the words we found. Words that rhyme have different beginning sounds, but the same middle and ending sounds. I'll show you. This word is _____. (Say a word from the list.) A word that rhymes with this word is _____. (Say a word that rhymes with the selected word.) Another word that rhymes with this word is _____. (Say a word that rhymes with the selected word.)

Listen to this word. (Point to and say another word from the list.) Who can think of a word that rhymes with _____? (elicit student responses) How about another word?

(Continue down the list and have students generate rhymes for each target word. Point out to students that rhymes don't have to be real words, they just have to have the same middle and ending sounds as the target word.)

Now let's tell Robbie some of the words.

(Call on each child to segment a word.)

Now listen to the words as Robbie says them. Tell me when you know which word he is saying.

(Say each word sound-by-sound—in random order—while students blend the words.)

That was good! Now we are going to read our passage one more time together. This time, when we come to one of the words with the (say target sound) sound, we'll say it sound-by-sound and then say the whole word.

(Read the passage with the students, stopping to segment and blend each word with the target sound.)

Good reading! Remember, when you are reading, that you can say a word sound-by-sound to figure out the word. Then, you can blend the sounds together to make the whole word.

Target Sound Word Lists

/m/
Pam
marshmallow
melt
moaned
mother
Mom
I'm
melting
must
make
move
Mister
moved
middle
room
more

/s/
Sue
silly
snake
hiss
sound
say
less
this
loose
search
said
miss
just
saw
slither
kiss
yes

/n/
Nina
and
Nona
twins
pennies
nickels
bank
bunny
ninety
ninety-nine
money

/p/
Pat
pedaled
pond
play
puppy
splashed
played
stopped
nap
pretty
supper
panted
perfect

/r/
Ralph
roared
roommate
Ronnie
there
more
roast
dinosaur
refrigerator
sorry
roar
grumpy
hungry
ran
store
for
roasted
another
dinner

/f/
four
funny
fish
first
found
frog
for
fork
friend
fling
fourth
forget
folks
furious
if
friends
fled
Fred
Floyd
Fran
Flo

/g/
ugly
bug
Wiggle
big
legs
good
great
goal
game
get
go
gate
got
hugs

/d/
Dolly
dog
could
dance
dart
dash
dip
dancer
dig
said
dumb
would
dangerous
did
didn't
ladder

/t/
Tom
told
to
front
store
went
bought
took
stomped
feet
turned
just
out
too
what
at

/a/	/e/	/o/	/u/	/i/
Jack	Meg	Mom	Bud	Kim
had	Ted	Bob	Gus	is
hat	sled	pop	club	big
Sam	read	popcorn	clubhouse	fish
sad	let	top	junk	lived
and	get	on	dump	dish
rack	yelled	popped	fun	Rick
asked	set	got	bun	live
glad	Help	hot	jug	fit
	next	dropped	but	in
	beds	mop	bus	six
	legs	mopped	jumped	did
		spot	up	flip
			begun	missed
				flipped
				with
				fin
				kiss

Pam the marshmallow began to melt.
Pam moaned to her mother, "Mom, I'm melting!
What must I do?"
Mom said, "Make a move away from the window.
Mister Sun won't be able to melt you."
Pam moved to the middle of the room.
Mister Sun passed by and the melting was no more.

Four funny fish swam in the pond.
Fred, the first fish, found a frog for dinner.
Floyd, the second fish, said "Fork it over, Fred!"
Fran, the third fish, said, "You're my friend, Fred, fling the
    frog to me."
Flo, the fourth fish, said, "Forget that frog, folks, he's mine."
All the arguing made Fred the fish furious.
Fred told the fish that he would share the frog if they could
    be friends again.
Just then, the frog fled and the funny fish had to find
    another dinner.

Sue had a silly snake named Monty.
Monty made a hiss sound when he was happy.
Sue told him to say less.
This made him mad.
One day, Monty got loose.
Sue began to search.
She said, "I miss Monty!"
Just then, she saw Monty slither to her.
Sue said, "I could kiss you! Yes, you can hiss all you want."

Pat pedaled to the pond.
She went to play with her puppy.
Pat and her puppy splashed and played in the pond.
They stopped awhile to nap by the pond, then they
    splashed some more.
Pretty soon, it was time for supper.
Pat pedaled home and her puppy panted along behind her.
It was a perfect day.

Ralph roared at his roommate, Ronnie.
There was no more roast dinosaur in the refrigerator.
Ronnie said, "I'm sorry. I ate all your roast dinosaur."
Ralph said, "I'm sorry to roar. I get so grumpy when I'm hungry."
Ronnie and Ralph ran to the store for more dinosaur.
The roommates roasted another dinosaur for dinner.

Nina and Nona are twins.
Nina likes pennies, but Nona likes nickels.
Nina's pennies are in a piggy bank.
Nona's nickels are in a bunny bank.
Nina has ninety-nine pennies.
Nona has ninety nickels.
Who has more money?

Once there was an ugly bug named Wiggle.
Wiggle had a lot of big hairy legs.
Wiggle was very good at games.
He was great at soccer.
Wiggle got a goal every game.
He could get the ball to go past the gate.
When Wiggle got a goal, he got a lot of hugs from
    other bugs.

Dolly was a dog that could dance.
Dolly would dart and dash and dip when she danced.
Dolly was a great dancer.
She would dance almost anywhere.
She could dig a hole and dance in it.
But she said she would never dance on a ladder.
Dolly was not a dumb dog!
She knew that would be dangerous.
She did dance a lot, but she didn't dance on ladders.

Tom told his friends to wait for him in front of the store.
He went in to buy some cookies.
Tom bought enough cookies for all of his friends.
He took the cookies to give to his friends, but they
    were gone.
Tom was so mad. He stomped his feet and his face
    turned red.
Just then, his friends came out of the store, too.
They handed Tom a soda and asked him what was wrong.
He just smiled at them. Now his face was red for another
    reason.

Jack had a big red hat.
Jack's friend Sam was sad because he had no hat.
Sam and Jack went to the hat rack to find a hat for Sam.
On the hat rack, Jack and Sam found a little blue hat.
The hat was too small for Sam's head.
Jack asked Sam if he wanted to try on the red hat.
Sam knew Jack's hat was the hat for him.
Sam gave Jack the blue hat.
They were both glad to have a new hat.

Meg and Ted took their sled to the top of the big hill.

They saw a sign that read "Do Not Sled."

Meg let Ted get on the sled.

They yelled, "Ready, set, go!"

Meg and Ted let the sled run until they spotted the cliff.

They yelled, "Help!"

The next thing they knew, Meg and Ted were in their
   beds with broken legs.

Kim is a big fish who lived in a big dish.

Rick came to live in the big dish with Kim.

Kim told Rick that two fish could not fit in the dish.

Rick told Kim that the dish was big enough for six fish.

Kim was so mad that she did a flip and almost missed
   the dish.

Rick flipped Kim back in with a fin.

Kim was so glad that she gave Rick a big kiss.

Mom and Bob wanted to pop popcorn.
Mom told Bob, "The top must be on tight."
The top was on so Bob popped and popped.
Bob got hungry for popcorn so he lifted the top.
It was too hot so Bob dropped the top.
Mom said, "Get the mop, Bob!"
When Bob had mopped the last spot, he got his popcorn.

Bud and Gus started a new club.
They built a clubhouse out of junk from the dump.
They had a lot of fun in their club.
They planned to sleep in the clubhouse, so Gus brought
    a bun and a jug of water.
But, Bud forgot his jug and his bun.
Bud took the bus to the store for a bun and a jug.
Bud jumped off the bus at the clubhouse.
Gus looked up and said, "Now the fun has really begun!"

GLOSSARY

Alphabetic principle: The understanding that there is a systematic relationship between letters and sounds

Blending: Combining sound units (syllables, onsets-rime, phonemes) together to form words

Consonant blend/consonant cluster: A combination of two or more adjacent consonants in which each retains its own sound (st, br, cl, sp)

Continuous sound: A sound that can be held out (f, l, m, n, r, s, v, z; all vowels) without distortion

Decoding: Converting print to speech by applying the alphabetic principle (i.e., the understanding of the systematic relationship between letters and sounds); refers to the process a reader uses to interpret abstract symbols as a unit that bears meaning

Digraph: Two letters written together that form one sound (sh, ch, th, ay, ea)

Diphthong: Two vowels or a vowel and a consonant combination that, when combined, produce a sound that "moves" or "glides" as it is pronounced (oi, ow)

Elision: A phonological skill that requires deleting a sound unit from a word. For example, "Say *meet*. Now say meet without saying /t/." [me]

Elkonin boxes: An approach developed by the Russian psychologist D. B. Elkonin, in which sound boxes are used to help children understand the relationship among individual sounds in words

Encoding: Converting speech to print by applying the alphabetic principle, (i.e., representing sounds in speech by appropriate graphemes). Spelling

Grapheme: A letter or letter combination that represents a spoken sound (i.e., phoneme). For example, the sound /z/ can be represented by the grapheme *z* (zebra) or *s* (is)

Invented spelling: Temporary unconventional spellings that children use in their attempts to write words. Invented spellings reflect the child's current level of phoneme segmentation ability and understanding of the alphabetic principle

Onset: In any syllable, the onset is the part of the syllable that precedes the vowel. In *meet,* the onset is /m/

Phoneme: The smallest unit of sound in spoken language

Phoneme manipulation: Performing various tasks at the phoneme level such as blending, segmenting, deleting, substituting, exchanging, or adding sounds in words

Phonemic awareness: The ability to reflect on and manipulate the sounds in language at the smallest unit of sound, the phoneme

Phonics: An instructional approach that focuses on the systematic relationship between letters and sounds, and how sounds map to letters to form words

Phonogram: Commonly used rimes from which multiple words can be formed (-at, -op, -ish, -eat)

Phonological awareness: The awareness that spoken language can be broken into smaller units such as words, syllables, onsets and rimes, and phonemes

Phonological recoding: The process of mapping speech sounds in written words to the corresponding graphemes and blending those sounds together to determine the appropriate pronunciation

Rhyme: Two words rhyme when they sound the same at middle and end of the word. That is, words share the same rime unit (*beet* and *feet; share* and *hair*)

Rime: In any syllable, the rime includes all the sounds from the vowel to the end of the syllable. In *meet,* the rime is eet

Schwa: A vowel or vowel digraph in an unstressed syllable, such as *a*bout or cert*ai*n

Segmenting: Breaking spoken language into smaller units of sound (sentences into words, words into syllables, onsets and rimes, or phonemes)

Stop sound: Sounds that cannot be held out (b, d, g, h, k, p, t)

Syllable: Units of speech that consist of at least a vowel, but usually other sound(s) before and/or after the vowel, as well (*bat, sis-ter, mo-tor-cy-cle*)

Unvoiced sound: A sound produced without vibrating vocal cords (/s/, /k/, /t/, /sh/)

Voiced sound: A sound produced, at least in part, by vibrating vocal cords as air moves past them (/m/, /b/, /z/)

Word family: A group of words formed from the same phonogram (cat, sat, mat, hat, vat)

REFERENCES

Adams, M. J. (1990). *Beginning to read: Thinking and learning about print.* Cambridge: MIT Press.

Adams, M. J. (2001). Alphabetic anxiety and explicit, systematic phonics instruction: A cognitive science perspective. In S. B. Neuman & D. K. Dickinson (Eds.), *Handbook of early literacy research* (pp. 66–80). New York: Guilford.

Adams, M. J., Foorman, B. R., Lundberg, I., & Beeler, T. (1998). *Phonemic awareness in young children: A classroom curriculum.* Baltimore: Paul H. Brookes.

Alegria, J., & Morais, J. (1991). Segmental analysis and reading acquisition. In L. Rieben & C. A. Perfetti (Eds.), *Learning to read: Basic research and its implications* (pp. 135–148). Hillsdale, NJ: Lawrence Erlbaum Associates.

Anderson, R. C., Hiebert, E. H., Scott, J. A., & Wilkinson, I. A. (1985). *Becoming a nation of readers: The report of the commission on reading.* Washington, D.C.: National Institute of Education.

Armbruster, B., Lehr, F., & Osborn, J. (2001). *Put reading first: The research building blocks for teaching children to read.* Washington, DC: National Institute for Literacy.

Badian, N. A. (1994). Preschool prediction: Orthographic and phonological skills, and reading. *Annals of Dyslexia, 44,* 3–25.

Badian, N. A. (1997). Dyslexia and the double deficit hypothesis. *Annals of Dyslexia, 47,* 69–87.

Ball, E. W., & Blachman, B. A. (1991). Does phoneme awareness training in kindergarten make a difference in early word recognition and developmental spelling? *Reading Research Quarterly, 26,* 49–66.

Barker, T., & Torgesen, J. (1995). An evaluation of computer-assisted instruction in phonological awareness with below average readers. *Journal of Educational Computing Research, 13,* 89–103.

Blachman, B. A. (1991). Early interventions for children's reading problems: Clinical applications of the research in phonological awareness. *Topics in Language Disorders, 12*(1), 51–65.

Blachman, B. A. (1994). What we have learned from longitudinal studies of phonological processing and reading, and some unanswered questions: A response to Torgesen, Wagner, and Rashotte. *Journal of Learning Disabilities, 27,* 287–291.

Blachman, B. A. (1995, March). *Identifying the core linguistic deficits and the critical conditions for early intervention with children with reading disabilities.* Paper presented at the annual meeting of the Learning Disabilities Association of America, Orlando, FL.

Blachman, B. A. (2000). Phonological awareness. In M. L. Kamil, P. B. Rosenthal, P. D. Pearson, & R. Barr (Eds.), *Handbook of reading research, Vol. III* (pp. 483–502). Mahwah, NJ: Lawrence Erlbaum Associates.

Blachman, B. A., Ball, E. W., Black, R., & Tangel, D. M. (2000). *Road to the code: A phonological awareness program for young children.* Baltimore: Paul H. Brookes.

Blachman, B. A., Tangel, D. M., Ball, E. W., Black, R., & McGraw, C. K. (1999). Developing phonological awareness and word-recognition skills: A two-year intervention with low-income, inner-city children. *Reading and Writing: An Interdisciplinary Journal, 11,* 239–273.

Bradley, L. (1988). Rhyme recognition and reading and spelling in young children. In R. L. Masland & M. W. Masland (Eds.), *Preschool prevention of reading failure* (pp. 143–162). Parkton, MD: York Press.

Bradley, L., & Bryant, P. E. (1983). Categorizing sounds and learning to read. *Nature, 301,* 419–421.

Brady, S. A. (1997). Ability to encode phonological representations: An underlying difficulty of poor readers. In B. Blachman (Ed.), *Foundations of reading acquisition and dyslexia: Implications for early intervention* (pp. 21–48). Mahwah, NJ: Erlbaum.

Bryant, P. E., MacLean, M., Bradley, L., & Crossland, J. (1990). Rhyme and alliteration, phoneme detection and learning to read. *Developmental Psychology, 26,* 429–438.

Bus, A., & van Ijzendoorn, M. (1999). Phonological awareness and early reading: A meta-analysis of experimental training studies. *Journal of Educational Psychology, 91,* 403–414.

Byrne, B., & Fielding-Barnsley, R. (1995). Evaluation of a program to teach phonemic awareness to young children. A 2- and 3-year follow up and a new preschool trial. *Journal of Educational Psychology, 87,* 488–503.

Calfee, R. C., Lindamood, P., & Lindamood, C. (1973). Acoustic-phonetic skills and reading: Kindergarten through twelfth grade. *Journal of Educational Psychology, 64,* 293–298.

Catts, H. W. (1986). Speech production/phonological deficits in reading-disordered children. *Journal of Learning Disabilities, 19,* 504–508.

Catts, H. W. (1991). Early identification of reading disabilities. *Topics in Language Disorders, 12*(1), 1–16.

Chard, D. J., & Dickson, S. V. (1999). Phonological awareness: Instructional and assessment guidelines. *Intervention in School and Clinic, 34,* 261–270.

Chard, D. J., & Osborn, J. (1999). Phonics and word recognition in early reading programs: Guidelines for accessibility. *Learning Disabilities Research and Practice, 14,* 107–117.

Chard, D. J., Simmons, D., & Kame'enui, E. (1998). Word recognition: Curricular and instructional implications for diverse learners. In D. C. Simmons & E. J. Kame'enui (Eds.), *What reading research tells us about children with diverse learning needs: Bases and basics* (pp. 143–167). Mahwah, NJ: Lawrence Erlbaum Associates.

Clay, M. (1993). *Reading Recovery: A guidebook for teachers in training.* Portsmouth, NH: Heinemann.

Cornwall, A. (1992). The relationship of phonological awareness, rapid naming, and verbal memory to severe reading and spelling disability. *Journal of Learning Disabilities, 25*(8), 532–538.

Cunningham, A. E. (1990). Explicit versus implicit instruction in phonemic awareness. *Journal of Experimental Child Psychology, 50,* 429–444.

Cunningham, P. M. (1999). *Phonics they use: Words for reading and writing* (3rd ed.). New York: Addison Wesley.

Ehri, L. C. (1989). The development of spelling knowledge and its role in reading acquisition and reading disability. *Journal of Learning Disabilities, 22,* 356–364.

Ehri, L. C. (1998). Grapheme-phoneme knowledge is essential for learning to read words in English. In J. L. Metsala & L. C. Ehri (Eds.), *Word recognition in beginning literacy* (pp. 3–40). Mahwah, NJ: Lawrence Erlbaum Associates.

Ehri, L. C., & Soffer, A. G. (1999). Graphophonemic awareness: Development in elementary students. *Scientific Studies of Reading, 3,* 1–30.

Elkonin, D. B. (1963). The psychology of mastering the elements of reading. In B. Simon & J. Simon (Eds.), *Educational psychology in the U.S.S.R.* (pp. 165–179). Stanford, CA: Stanford University Press.

Erikson, G. C., Foster, K. C., Foster, D. F., & Torgesen, J. K. (1992). *Daisy Quest.* Austin, TX: Pro-Ed.

Erikson, G. C., Foster, K. C., Foster, D. F., & Torgesen, J. K. (1993). *Daisy's Castle.* Austin, TX: Pro-Ed.

Fawcett, A., & Nicholson, R. (1994). Naming speed in children with dyslexia. *Journal of Learning Disabilities, 27,* 641–646.

Fielding-Barnsley, R. (1997). Explicit instruction in decoding benefits children high in phonemic awareness and alphabet knowledge. *Scientific Studies of Reading, 1,* 85–98.

Ganske, K. (2000). *Word journeys: Assessment-guided phonics, spelling, and vocabulary instruction.* New York: Guilford.

Haskell, D. W., Foorman, B. R., & Swank, P. R. (1992). Effects of three orthographic/phonological units on first-grade reading. *Remedial and Special Education, 13,* 40–49.

Hatcher, P. J., & Hulme, C. (1999). Phonemes, rhymes, and intelligence as predictors of children's responsiveness to remedial reading instruction: Evidence from a longitudinal intervention study. *Journal of Experimental Child Psychology, 72,* 130–153.

Hatcher, P. J., Hulme, C., & Ellis, A. W. (1994). Ameliorating early reading failure by integrating the teaching of reading and phonological awareness skills: The phonological linkage hypothesis. *Child Development, 65,* 41–57.

Hayes, L. F., Lane, H. B., & Pullen, P. C. (1999). *University of Florida literacy initiative: Tutoring for beginning readers.* Gainesville, FL: University of Florida.

Herron, J., Sabbag, L., & Rechis, M. (1995). *Read, write, and type.* Fremont, CA: The Learning Company.

Invernizzi, M., & Meier, J. (2001). *Phonological awareness and literacy screening: 1–3.* Charlottesville, VA: University of Virginia.

Invernizzi, M., Meier, J., Swank, L. K., & Juel, C. (1998). *Phonological awareness and literacy screening—Kindergarten.* Charlottesville, VA: University of Virginia.

Invernizzi, M., Sullivan, A., & Meier, J. (2001). *Phonological awareness and literacy screening—PreK.* Charlottesville, VA: University of Virginia.

Iversen, S., & Tunmer, W. E. (1993). Phonological processing skills and the Reading Recovery Program. *Journal of Educational Psychology, 85,* 112–126.

Joseph, L. M. (2000). Using word boxes as a large group phonics approach in a first grade classroom. *Reading Horizons, 41,* 117–127.

Juel, C., Griffith, P. L., & Gough, P. B. (1986) Acquisition of literacy: A longitudinal study of children in first and second grade. *Journal of Educational Psychology, 78,* 243–255.

Kamhi, A., & Catts, H. (1989). *Reading disabilities: A developmental language perspective.* Austin, TX: Pro-ED.

Kaminski, R. A., & Good, R. H. (1996). Toward a technology for assessing basic early literacy skills. *School Psychology Review, 25,* 215–227.

Kroese, J. M., Hynd, G. W., Knight, D. F., Hall, J., & Hiemenz, J. R. (2000). Clinical appraisal of spelling ability and its relationship to phonemic awareness (blending, segmenting, elision, and reversal), phonological memory, and reading in reading disabled, ADHD, and normal children. *Reading and Writing: An Interdisciplinary Journal, 13,* 105–131.

Lane, H. B. (1994). *The effects of explicit instruction in contextual application of phonological awareness on the reading skills of first-grade students.* Unpublished doctoral dissertation. University of Florida, Gainesville, FL.

Lane, H. B., Pullen, P. C., Eisele, M. R., & Jordan, L. (2002). Preventing reading failure: Phonological awareness assessment and instruction. *Preventing School Failure, 46*(3) 101–110.

Lane, H. B., Pullen, P. C., & Hudson, R. F. (2003). Identifying essential elements of literacy tutoring for struggling beginning readers. Unpublished manuscript.

Lenchner, O., Gerber, M. M., & Routh, D. K. (1990). Phonological awareness tasks as predictors of decoding ability: Beyond segmentation. *Journal of Learning Disabilities, 23*(4), 240–247.

Liberman, I., & Shankweiler, D. (1985). Phonology and the problems of learning to read and write. *Remedial and Special Education, 6,* 8–17.

Liberman, I. Y., & Shankweiler, D. (1991). Phonology and beginning reading: A tutorial. In L. Rieben & C. A. Perfetti (Eds.), *Learning to read: Basic research and its implications* (pp. 3–17). Hillsdale, NJ: Lawrence Erlbaum Associates.

Liberman, I.Y., Shankweiler, D., Fischer, F. W., & Carter, B. (1974). Explicit syllable and phoneme segmentation in young children. *Journal of Experimental Child Psychology, 18,* 201–212.

Liberman, I. Y., Shankweiler, D., & Liberman, A. M. (1989). The alphabetic principle and learning to read. In D. Shankweiler & I. Y. Liberman (Eds.), *Phonology and reading disability: Solving the reading puzzle* (pp. 1–33). Ann Arbor: The University of Michigan Press.

Lindamood, C. H., & Lindamood, P. C. (1975). *The A.D.D. program: Auditory discrimination in depth.* Hingham, MA: Teaching Resources Corporation.

Lindamood, C. H., & Lindamood, P. C. (1979). *Lindamood Auditory Conceptualization Test.* Austin, TX: Pro-ED.

Lundberg, I. (1988). Preschool prevention of reading failure: Does training in phonological awareness work? In R. L. Masland & M. W. Masland (Eds.), *Preschool prevention of reading failure* (pp. 163–176). Parkton, MD: York Press.

Lundberg, I., Frost, J., & Petersen, O. (1988). Effects of an extensive program for stimulating phonological awareness in preschool children. *Reading Research Quarterly, 23,* 263–284.

MacLean, M., Bryant, P., & Bradley, L. (1987). Rhymes, nursery rhymes, and reading in early childhood. *Merrill-Palmer Quarterly, 33,* 255–281.

Mann, V. (1986). Why some children encounter reading problems: The contribution of difficulties with language processing and phonological sophistication to early reading disability. In J. Torgesen & B. Wong (Eds.), *Psychological and educational perspectives on learning disabilities* (pp. 133–159). New York: Academic Press.

Mann, V. A. (1991). Phonological abilities: Effective predictors of future reading ability. In L. Rieben & C. A. Perfetti (Eds.), *Learning to read: Basic research and its implications* (pp. 121–133). Hillsdale, NJ: Lawrence Erlbaum Associates.

Mann, V. A. (1993). Phoneme awareness and future reading ability. *Journal of Learning Disabilities, 26*(4), 259–269.

Mann, V. A., Tobin, P., & Wilson, R. (1987). Measuring phonological awareness through the invented spellings of kindergarten children. *Merrill-Palmer Quarterly, 33,* 365–391.

McBride-Chang, C. M. (1995). What is phonological awareness? *Journal of Educational Psychology, 87*(2), 179–192.

McGuiness, D., McGuiness, C., & Donohue, J. (1995). Phonological training and the alphabet principle: Evidence for reciprocal causality. *Reading Research Quarterly, 30,* 830–852.

Mercer, C. D., Lane, H. B., Jordan, L., Allsopp, D. H., & Eisele, M. R. (1996). Empowering students and teachers with instructional choices in inclusive settings. *Remedial and Special Education, 17,* 226–236.

Mercer, C. D., & Miller, S. P. (1992). Teaching students with learning problems in math to acquire, understand, and apply basic math facts. *Remedial and Special Education, 13*(3), 19–35, 61.

Merzenich, M., Tallal, P., Jenkins, W., & Miller, S. (1996). *Fast ForWord.* Oakland, CA: Scientific Learning.

Morais, J., Mousty, P., & Kolinsky, R. (1998). Why and how phoneme awareness helps learning to read. In C. Hulme and R.M. Joshi (Eds.), *Reading and spelling: Development and disorders.* (pp. 127–152). Mahwah, NJ: Lawrence Erlbaum Associates.

Morris, D., & Perney, J. (1984). Developmental spelling as a predictor of first-grade reading achievement. *Elementary School Journal, 84,* 441–457.

National Reading Panel. (2000). *Teaching children to read: An evidence-based assessment of the scientific research literature on reading and its implications for reading instruction.* Washington, DC: National Institute of Child Health and Human Development.

Notari-Syverson, A., O'Connor, R. E., & Vadasy, P. F. (1998). *Ladders to literacy: A preschool activity book.* Baltimore: Paul H. Brookes.

O'Connor, R. E., Jenkins, J. R., Leicester, N., & Slocum, T. A. (1993). Teaching phonological awareness to young children with learning disabilities. *Exceptional Children, 59,* 532–546.

O'Connor, R. E., Notari-Syverson, A., & Vadasy, P. F. (1998). *Ladders to literacy: A kindergarten activity book.* Baltimore: Paul H. Brookes.

Perfetti, C. A. (1991). Representations and awareness in the acquisition of reading competence. In L. Rieben & C. A. Perfetti (Eds.), *Learning to read: Basic research and its implications* (pp. 33–44). Hillsdale, NJ: Lawrence Erlbaum Associates.

Perfetti, C. A., Beck, I., Bell, L. C., & Hughes, C. (1987). Phonemic knowledge and learning to read are reciprocal: A longitudinal study of first grade children. *Merrill-Palmer Quarterly, 33,* 283–319.

Pratt, A. C., & Brady, S. (1988). Relation of phonological awareness to reading disability in children and adults. *Journal of Educational Psychology, 80*(3), 319–323.

Pullen, P. C. (2000). *The effects of alphabetic word work with manipulative letters on the reading acquisition of struggling first-grade students.* Unpublished doctoral dissertation. University of Florida, Gainesville, FL.

Reitsma, P., & Wesseling, R. (1998). Effects of computer-assisted training of blending skills in kindergartners. *Scientific Studies of Reading, 2,* 301–320.

Smith, S., Simmons, D., & Kame'enui, E. (1998). Phonological awareness: Curricular and instructional implications for diverse learners. In D. C. Simmons & E. J. Kame'enui (Eds.), *What reading research tells us about children with diverse learning needs: Bases and basics* (pp. 129–140). Mahwah, NJ: Lawrence Erlbaum Associates.

Snow, C. E., Burns, M. S., & Griffin, P. (Eds.). (1998). *Preventing reading difficulties in young children.* Washington, D.C.: National Academy Press.

Stahl, S. A. (2002). Teaching phonics and phonological awareness. In S. B. Neuman & D. K. Dickinson (Eds.), *Handbook of early literacy research* (pp. 333–360). New York: Guilford.

Stahl, S. A., & Murray, B. A. (1994). Defining phonological awareness and its relationship to early reading. *Journal of Educational Psychology, 86*(2), 221–234.

Stanovich, K. E. (1986a). Cognitive processes and the reading problems of learning disabled children: Evaluating the assumption of specificity. In J. K. Torgesen & B. Y. L. Wong (Eds.), *Psychological and educational perspectives on learning disabilities* (pp. 87–131). New York: Academic Press.

Stanovich, K. E. (1986b). Matthew effects in reading: Some consequences of individual differences in the acquisition of literacy. *Reading Research Quarterly, 21,* 360–406.

Stanovich, K. E. (1987). Introduction to special issue. *Merrill-Palmer Quarterly, 33.*

Stanovich, K. E. (1992). Speculations on the causes and consequences of individual differences in early reading acquisition. In P. B. Gough, L. C. Ehri, & R. Treiman (Eds.), *Reading acquisition* (pp. 307–342). Hillsdale, NJ: Lawrence Erlbaum Associates.

Tangel, D. M., & Blachman, B. A. (1992). Effect of phoneme awareness instruction on kindergarten children's invented spelling. *Journal of Reading Behavior, 24,* 233–256.

Tangel, D. M., & Blachman, B. A. (1995). Effect of phoneme awareness instruction on the invented spelling of first-grade children: A one-year follow-up. *Journal of Reading Behavior, 27,* 153–185.

Torgesen, J. K., & Barker, T. A. (1995). Computers as aids in the prevention and remediation of reading disabilities. *Learning Disability Quarterly, 18,* 76–87.

Torgesen, J. K., & Bryant, B. R. (1994). *Phonological awareness training for reading.* Austin, TX: Pro-ed.

Torgesen, J. K., Morgan, S. T., & Davis, C. (1992). Effects of two types of phonological awareness training on word learning in kindergarten children. *Journal of Educational Psychology, 84,* 364–370.

Torgesen, J. K., Wagner, R. K., Bryant, B. R., & Pearson, N. (1992). Toward development of a kindergarten group test for phonological awareness. *Journal of Research and Development in Education, 25,* 113–120.

Torgesen, J. K., Wagner, R. K., & Rashotte, C. A. (1997). Prevention and remediation of severe reading disabilities: Keeping the end in mind. *Scientific Studies of Reading, 1,* 217–234.

Treiman, R. (1985). Onsets and rimes as units of spoken syllables: Evidence from children. *Journal of Experimental Child Psychology, 39,* 161–181.

Treiman, R. (1991). The role of intrasyllabic units in learning to read. In L. Rieben & C. A. Perfetti (Eds.), *Learning to read: Basic research and its implications* (pp. 149–160). Hillsdale, NJ: Lawrence Erlbaum Associates.

Treiman, R. (1992). The role of intrasyllabic units in learning to read and spell. In P. B. Gough, L. C. Ehri, & R. Treiman (Eds.), *Reading acquisition* (pp. 65–106). Hillsdale, NJ: Lawrence Erlbaum Associates.

Treiman, R., & Bourassa, D. C. (2000). The development of spelling skill. *Topics in Language Disorders, 20*(3), 1–18.

Vellutino, F. R., & Scanlon, D. M. (1987). Phonological coding, phonological awareness, and reading ability: Evidence from a longitudinal and experimental study. *Merrill-Palmer Quarterly, 33,* 321–363.

Wagner, R. K., & Torgesen, J. K. (1987). The nature of phonological processing and its causal role in the acquisition of reading skills. *Psychological Bulletin, 101,* 192–212.

Wagner, R., Torgesen, J., & Rashotte, C. (1999). *Comprehensive test of phonological processing* (CTOPP). Austin, TX: Pro-Ed.

Wasowicz, J. (1997). *Earobics 1.* Evanston, IL: Cognitive Concepts.

Wasowicz, J. (1999). *Earobics 2.* Evanston, IL: Cognitive Concepts.

Waterford Institute. (1993). *Waterford early learning program.* Sunnyvale, CA: Electronic Education.

Wesseling, R., & Reitsma, P. (2000). The transient role of explicit phonological recoding for reading acquisition. *Reading and Writing: An Interdisciplinary Journal, 13,* 313–336.

Wise, B., King, J., & Olson, R. (2000). Individual differences in benefits from computer-assisted remedial reading. *Journal of Experimental Child Psychology, 77,* 197–235.

Wolf, M. (1997). A provisional, integrative account of phonological and naming-speed deficits in dyslexia: Implications for diagnosis and intervention. In B. Blachman (Ed.), *Foundations of reading acquisition and dyslexia: Implications for early intervention* (pp. 67–92). Mahwah, NJ: Lawrence Erlbaum Associates.

Yopp, H. K. (1988). The validity and reliability of phonemic awareness tests. *Reading Research Quarterly, 23,* 159–177.

Yopp, H. K. (1992). Developing phonemic awareness in young children. *The Reading Teacher, 45,* 696–703.

Index